THE SEX HABITS OF AMERICAN WOMEN was first produced by the Magic Theater, San Francisco, opening on 11 October 2003. The cast and creative contributors were:

DAUGHTER . . . . Stephanie Champion
JOY . . . . Anne Darragh
DAISY . . . . .Deborah Fink
AGNES . . . . Frances Lee McCain
DR FRITZ TITTELS . . . . Jarion Monroe
RUBY . . . . Rebecca Noon
EDGAR . . . . Kevin Rolston
DAN . . . . .Mark Routhier

Director . . . . Michael Bigelow Dixon
Video director . . . . Amy Glazer
Set & light design . . . . .Kate Boyd
Costume design . . . . Todd Roehrman
Director of photography . . . . Rob Humphrey
Video & sound design/special effects . . . . .Michael Woody
Video sound design . . . . Brian Copenhagen
Production manager . . . . Kenny Bell
Stage manager . . . . Milton Commons
Casting director . . . . Jessica Heidt
Line producers . . . . Regan Gradet & Jessica Heidt
Props, wardrobe, make-up . . . . Sarah Ellen Joynt

CHARACTERS & SETTING

AGNES TITTELS, *mid-sixties; wife to* DOCTOR FRITZ TITTELS.

DOCTOR FRITZ TITTELS, *mid-sixties. German psychoanalyst writing the book* The Sex Habits of American Women.

DAISY TITTELS, *thirty-five; daughter of* AGNES *and* FRITZ. *Unmarried.*

EDGAR GREEN, *early thirties. Young psychoanalyst.* DR TITTELS's *former student.*

RUBY LAWRENCE, *twenties.* DAISY's *friend.*

JOY, *seen only on video. Fifty. Sexy. Contemporary.*

KATIE, JOY's *daughter, seen only on video. A teenager. Contemporary.*

DAN, *cameraman/interviewer of documentary on T V. Seen only once, from behind...from a distance. Contemporary.*

Place: New York, NY

Setting: 1950. Stage to be very stylized. Late 40s furniture, clothes, colors, mood. (As if lifted from an old advertisement for "the good life" as presented by a cleaning product in Life *magazine.)*

THE SEX HABITS OF AMERICAN WOMEN

Julie Marie Myatt

BROADWAY PLAY PUBLISHING INC
224 E 62nd St, NY, NY 10065
www.broadwayplaypub.com
info@broadwayplaypub.com

THE SEX HABITS OF AMERICAN WOMEN
© Copyright 2008 by Julie Marie Myatt

First printing: May 2008, Second printing: June 2015
I S B N: 978-0-88145-378-2

Book design: Marie Donovan
Word processing: Microsoft Word
Typographic controls: Ventura Publisher
Typeface: Palatino
Printed and bound in the U S A

ACT ONE

(On the screen, in black and white, a woman, JOY, *opens the front door of her modest house. The interviewer/cameraman is invisible. It's 2004. The camera moves in closer.)*

JOY: *(On video)* You're making a what?... *(She laughs...fixes her hair)*

DAN: *(Offscreen)* A documentary on the Sex Habits of American Women.

JOY: Really? ...And you think I'm gonna tell the truth?

(The screen fades to black.)

(1950)

SCENE ONE:
INTRODUCTION

*(*AGNES TITTELS *sits on the couch, reading a book.)*

*(*DOCTOR FRITZ TITTELS *sits before his typewriter excitedly working on the introduction of his book.)*

(There is a great distance between them.)

DOCTOR TITTELS: "To begin to understand a woman's relationship to sex is to begin to understand that she cannot be understood. Alas, she is a paradox. All the flowers in the world or whispers in the ear will not reveal what she craves most: *Love*. While sexual fulfillment is indeed valuable to her, her needs for love and affection far outweigh those of erotic bliss. Love is often lost in our harried drive for cold hard cash and the noisy hustle and bustle we call our modern world, but it cannot be compromised or underestimated in regards to an American woman because it is ultimately where we *can* begin to understand her. Love is the screw that opens her Pandora's box." *(He waits. And waits)* Agnes?

AGNES: Yes, dear?

DOCTOR TITTELS: What do you think?

AGNES: About what, dear?

DOCTOR TITTELS: My book. Weren't you listening?

AGNES: Of course I was.

(DOCTOR TITTELS waits.)

DOCTOR TITTELS: Well?

(AGNES thinks. Finally)

AGNES: I don't like "hustle and bustle". *(She returns to her book.)*

DOCTOR TITTELS: Why not?

AGNES: Sounds like some kind of teenager wrote it.

DOCTOR TITTELS: Does it?

AGNES: Yes.

DOCTOR TITTELS: "Hustle and bustle"?

AGNES: Yes.

(DOCTOR TITTELS reads it over again, worried.)

DOCTOR TITTELS: I like it. *(He waits.)*

AGNES: It's your book, dear.

DOCTOR TITTELS: Of course it is. And anyone who knows anything about my work knows I am indeed not a teenager.

AGNES: Indeed.

DOCTOR TITTELS: You don't ask one of the world's leading psychoanalysts to write a book on his expertise and then call him a teenager.

AGNES: Who called you a teenager dear?

DOCTOR TITTELS: You did—

AGNES: Did I ask you to write the book? *(She continues reading.)*

(DOCTOR TITTELS returns to his work.)

DOCTOR TITTELS: The introduction is very important. It must both draw in the reader and introduce my theories. This is a major work, Agnes. Not to be cast aside lightly.

AGNES: Of course not.

DOCTOR TITTELS: Ground-breaking material here.

(AGNES checks her watch, stands, sets aside her book.)

DOCTOR TITTELS: You could be a bit more—

AGNES: We're having roast for dinner.

DOCTOR TITTELS: Fine.

AGNES: Daisy's coming.

DOCTOR TITTELS: Is she?

AGNES: She's bringing a friend.

DOCTOR TITTELS: Oh. Do I know him?

AGNES: I don't know, dear.

DOCTOR TITTELS: You don't know?

AGNES: No. I guess I don't.

DOCTOR TITTELS: Why not?

AGNES: With all the hustle and bustle, I forgot to ask.

(DOCTOR TITTELS *returns to his papers. Makes a quick correction*)

DOCTOR TITTELS: "Many women wake up one day and realize that they are married to a man that they no longer love. They realize that he has become indifferent, self-involved, cruel, or has become more interested in the lure of libations than Love—

AGNES: Another cocktail dear? (*She offers a bottle of scotch.*)

DOCTOR TITTELS: "They feel unrequited, lonely, and would indeed consider leaving him were it not for the fact that they are financially dependent and they have no way to provide for themselves—

AGNES: Fritz?

DOCTOR TITTELS: "What is left for these women when they discover this dark chasm in their marriage? What kind of life do they see before them?"

(AGNES *exits without refilling* DOCTOR TITTELS's *drink.*)

(DOCTOR TITTELS *finally looks up from his work.*)

DOCTOR TITTELS: Yes?

(*On the video screen,* JOY *sits in a chair, looking at the camera.*)

DAN: (O S) When was the last time you were married?

JOY: Do you mind if I smoke?

DAN: *(O S)* No—

JOY: Have you ever been married?

DAN: *(O S)* No.

JOY: Why not?

DAN: *(O S)* I don't know—

JOY: Afraid?

DAN: *(O S)* No—

JOY: Never fall in love?

DAN: *(O S)* No, could you just—

JOY: Afraid of being rejected?

DAN: *(O S)* No. Please. Could you just answer my question—

JOY: It is very hard to say "no" to someone with a diamond in his hand—

DAN: *(O S)* The last time—

JOY: It's a very shiny, distracting object...remember that.

DAN: *(O S)* The last time you were married?

JOY: Four years ago.

DAN: *(O S)* Four years. Thank you. And the sex?

JOY: We were not very compatible. That way.

DAN: *(O S)* He was a bad lover.

JOY: He was fine...when he was high...but otherwise he was as uptight as a fucking Mormon...I had been married before that too, but...

DAN: *(O S)* Did your sex life affect *that* marriage?

JOY: It was the best I've ever had.

DAN: *(O S)* Then why'd it end?

JOY: He left me.

DAN: *(O S)* Oh... Why'd he leave you?

JOY: Have you ever left someone?

DAN: *(O S)* We're not talking about me—

JOY: Commitment issues—

DAN: *(O S)* It just wasn't working.

JOY: See...

DAN: *(O S)* But the sex was average, and we weren't married.

JOY: Great sex can't save a dead marriage.

(Slam of a door O S. JOY looks at her watch.)

JOY: My daughter.

DAN: *(O S)* Can kids?

JOY: Can kids what?

DAN: *(O S)* Save a marriage?

(KATIE, fifteen, walks in behind them.)

JOY: Say hello to the camera, Katie. Mom's giving away all her dirty little secrets.

(Both the camera and JOY follow her daughter as she rolls her eyes and avoids the camera.)

JOY: He wants to know if kids can save a marriage.

KATIE: Tell him to ask a normal person. *(She slams the bathroom door.)*

JOY: Did you see that?

DAN: *(O S)* What?

(The camera moves to JOY's face.)

JOY: *(Laughing)* Her shirt was not only inside out. It was on backwards!

(The camera follows JOY as she walks to the bathroom door and knocks.)

JOY: Hey Katie...looks like you two got a lot of studying done...

KATIE: *(O S)* Uh huh.

JOY: Guess that means you'll get an A on the test tomorrow?

SCENE TWO:
THE GIRL IN THE FAMILY

(DAISY *enters and surveys the room. She makes herself a drink and takes a seat.*)

(AGNES *enters with her hat and coat.*)

AGNES: Daisy. What a nice surprise... How are you?

(DAISY *stares at her mother.*)

AGNES: Wonderful. Well, I'm just on my way out, dear—

(DAISY *hands her mother a crumpled piece of paper.*)

DAISY: That was passed around the entire school.

(AGNES *reads it.*)

DAISY: Every student got a chance to add a clever comment.

AGNES: What do you care about them.

DAISY: Or an illustration. Look how they drew me, Mother.

AGNES: It looks nothing like you. You are thin, but those fangs and that hair really are way out of proportion—

DAISY: "Old Maid Tittels."

AGNES: You know you're a fine teacher, Daisy—

DAISY: "Old Maid." "Lives in a shoe, can't find a husband, so she's stuck teaching you."

AGNES: It's a silly note.

DAISY: I hate children.

AGNES: You know that's not true.

DAISY: Giggling vultures.

AGNES: You wanted to be a teacher.

DAISY: I wanted to be Flash Gordon—

AGNES: Please-

DAISY: But his rocket was full.

AGNES: That joke wasn't funny the first time, Daisy, and it's never been funny since. You wanted to be a teacher—

DAISY: Same could be said for your nagging, Mother.

AGNES: I'm not nagging.

(DAISY *takes back her note.*)

DAISY: Oh, but I can hear it coming. Like a train whistling around the bend. It's not far.

(Silence)

AGNES: We missed you at dinner last night.

DAISY: All aboard.

AGNES: Well, I would have cooked for two, not four—

DAISY: He stood me up.

AGNES: What?

DAISY: He dumped me.

AGNES: Already?

DAISY: Already.

AGNES: Just like that?

DAISY: Just like that.

AGNES: Another one?

DAISY: Come and gone.

AGNES: My goodness.

DAISY & AGNES: Sakes.

(Silence)

AGNES: Why buy the cow...

DAISY: Milk has nothing to do with it.

(Silence)

AGNES: You don't try hard enough, Daisy.

DAISY: You're right.

AGNES: You could use a haircut. And look at that dress.
I bought you an iron, didn't I?

DAISY: I just need to try harder.

AGNES: I think your students are very observant.
I mean, did any of them draw a smile on your face?

DAISY: My fangs are turned upward.

AGNES: You could try and learn a thing or two from
them.

DAISY: What?

AGNES: Enthusiasm? Exuberance?

DAISY: I'm thirty-five.

AGNES: You don't need to remind me.

(Silence. DAISY gathers herself.)

DAISY: I've tried everything.

AGNES: Well, you always have been a terrible
underachiever, dear. Your style of "trying" might
not stand up well against other girls—

DAISY: Hairspray, new dresses, manicures, etiquette
classes, French perfume, I'm wearing not one but two
padded bras—I'm a woman, Mom.

AGNES: I know—

DAISY: I'm too old to be like other 'girls.'

AGNES: You *are* still coming home to cry on your mother's shoulder.

(DAISY *pours herself another drink. Toasts her mother*)

DAISY: Sympathy will never be your strong suit, Mother.

AGNES: I was eighteen when I married your father.

DAISY: So?

AGNES: I really don't know how to help you, dear.

DAISY: You married him and lost all capacity to imagine anything else?

AGNES: Yes.

DAISY: You're lying.

AGNES: Don't speak to me that way, Daisy. I don't appreciate it. *(Silence)* You fritter away your opportunities with men, Daisy. Always have. Then you come here and want me to pat your head and build you back up again. Well, maybe next time if you try and act a little more young, and carefree, and charming, and less like a bitter old schoolmarm, you might just get a ring on your finger.

DAISY: Would that make you happy?

AGNES: No.

DAISY: Then what's the point?

AGNES: Your happiness, dear.

DAISY: That's right.

DOCTOR TITTELS: *(O S)* Agnes?

DAISY: And Dad's.

AGNES: Yes. His too—

(DOCTOR TITTELS *enters with a stack of papers.*)

DOCTOR TITTELS: Listen to this—

AGNES: I really am late, dear—

DOCTOR TITTELS: "When the sexual urge makes its powerful march on the female psyche at puberty, the budding woman begins to seek counsel with her new best friend: Desire. (It will be a troubled friendship)—

AGNES: Wonderful. The forty dollars?

DOCTOR TITTELS: Oh, hello Daisy.

DAISY: Daddy.

DOCTOR TITTELS: Where were you last night?

DAISY: Out kicking up my heels like a cheerful young girl.

AGNES: Alright, Daisy—

DOCTOR TITTELS: Well, you could have called.

DAISY: I was too busy being enthusiastic.

DOCTOR TITTELS: Your mother cooked a fantastic meal for you and your friend, what's his name...what's his name?

DAISY: It's not important.

DOCTOR TITTELS: Your mother put out the nice china and the candles and so forth, and we had to just sit there and watch it get cold.

DAISY: I apologize.

AGNES: The forty dollars, Fritz?

DAISY: But you didn't have to just sit there and watch it get cold.

DOCTOR TITTELS: What were we supposed to do?

DAISY: You've got that Ph.D, Daddy. Couldn't you and Mother put your heads together and come up with something?

AGNES: The forty dollars—

DOCTOR TITTELS: We've got manners—

AGNES: Fritz?

DOCTOR TITTELS: What for?

AGNES: I told you what for. I need to buy groceries and I'm having lunch with my sister.

DOCTOR TITTELS: You could use some manners, Daisy.

(DOCTOR TITTELS *hands* AGNES *a twenty. She keeps her hand out.*)

DOCTOR TITTELS: That is plenty.

AGNES: But I said forty, dear. Don't make a fuss.

DOCTOR TITTELS: A phone call would have been considerate, right Agnes? (*He hands over the money.*)

AGNES: Yes, dear.

(AGNES *hands a twenty to* DAISY.)

AGNES: Go buy yourself something pretty, Daisy.

DAISY: That's O K, Mother.

AGNES: Just a little something. It'll make you look, and feel better.

DOCTOR TITTELS: What kind of message does that send, Agnes? She was rude and now we give her money?

DAISY: I promise all your "messages" as parents have been well sent and received by now, Daddy.

AGNES: Her boyfriend dumped her, Fritz. And her students think she's a outcast—

DOCTOR TITTELS: I told her those public schools don't pay squat. She didn't listen to me, no—

DAISY: I don't need the money.

DOCTOR TITTELS: She could be a professor by now, but no, she's too lazy.

AGNES: I wish I had had those kinds of opportunities and encouragement when I was—

DOCTOR TITTELS: She doesn't listen.

DAISY: I don't want the money!

DOCTOR TITTELS & AGNES: Fine.

(DOCTOR TITTELS *takes the money.*)

DOCTOR TITTELS: If I had a penny for every bit of good advice Daisy ignored, I'd be a millionaire eating coconuts for breakfast.

(AGNES *takes the money back. She adjusts her hat.*)

AGNES: Pull yourself together, Daisy.

(DAISY *just stares at her mother.*)

AGNES: Good-bye, Fritz.

(AGNES *exits. Leaving* DOCTOR TITTELS *and* DAISY *alone with little to say to each other. They look at each other. Push fake smiles. Without* AGNES, *there's a void. He finally gathers his papers.*)

DAISY: How's the "thesis" coming?

DOCTOR TITTELS: It's a book, Daisy.

DAISY: Book.

(DOCTOR TITTELS *doesn't respond.*)

DAISY: How's the stupid book?

DOCTOR TITTELS: You won't think it's so stupid when it's buying your inheritance.

DAISY: That's all I need...sex money.

DOCTOR TITTELS: *Psychological* studies—

DAISY: "The little panties tell all."

DOCTOR TITTELS: Scientific facts—

DAISY: "The fantasies of housewives revealed."

(DOCTOR TITTELS begins to exit, then stops.)

DOCTOR TITTELS: I would prefer to have an adult relationship with my daughter from time to time.

DAISY: Maybe if you treated her like an adult you might have a chance.

DOCTOR TITTELS: I treat you like an adult.

DAISY: Doesn't feel like it.

DOCTOR TITTELS: Your mother has spoiled you. Nothing is ever enough for you, Daisy. You take take take.

DAISY: Maybe I need need need.

DOCTOR TITTELS: I don't know what happened. We were textbook parents and look at you. *(He exits.)*

DAISY: Someone should burn that book.

(On the video screen, JOY is showing her bedroom to the camera.)

DAN: *(O S)* Bed's kind of small.

JOY: I like a smaller bed. Those king sizes are fine, but I think they tempt couples apart.

DAN: *(O S)* How?

JOY: You could drive a truck between the two of you. There's a thousand things you don't have to deal with when you can just roll over into your oasis over there... I like to breathe down the neck of my men. Smother them until they have to have me.

DAN: *(O S)* Isn't a little space important?

JOY: He can sleep at his house if he wants space.

SCENE THREE:
IN LOVE WITH HERSELF

(The TITTLES *living room)*

*(*AGNES *enters and looks around the room. It is empty. She closes the door behind her, leans on it and smiles. Dreamy, tipsy and happy)*

DOCTOR TITTELS: *(O S)* Agnes, is that you? Agnes? *(He enters, a pile of notes in his hands.)*

DOCTOR TITTELS: Did you hear me?

AGNES: Yes, dear.

DOCTOR TITTELS: Why didn't you answer?

AGNES: I don't know.

DOCTOR TITTELS: I'm missing chapter five.

AGNES: Are you?

DOCTOR TITTELS: Have you seen it?

AGNES: I don't know.

DOCTOR TITTELS: You don't know?

AGNES: No.

DOCTOR TITTELS: Chapter five.

AGNES: What about it, dear?

DOCTOR TITTELS: Have you seen it?

AGNES: I don't know.

DOCTOR TITTELS: Chapter Five.

AGNES: What's it look like?

DOCTOR TITTELS: A stack of papers.

AGNES: What kind of papers?

DOCTOR TITTELS: Called "The Frigid Woman".

AGNES: I don't know her. *(She struggles to take off her coat. Her arm gets caught in the sleeve and she leaves it on.)*

DOCTOR TITTELS: Where are the groceries?

(AGNES tries to remove her hat and can't get it off either. She decides to tip her head upside down to help it fall off.)

AGNES: I haven't seen them either.

DOCTOR TITTELS: Have you seen your wits?

AGNES: No, I don't think so, dear. *(She laughs, steadies herself on a wall.)* Oh my...

DOCTOR TITTELS: You're drunk.

(AGNES shakes her head, laughing.)

AGNES: Am I?

DOCTOR TITTELS: Completely inebriated.

AGNES: You exaggerate.

DOCTOR TITTELS: I saw you lean against the wall there.

AGNES: Did you?

DOCTOR TITTELS: I did.

AGNES: Did I?

DOCTOR TITTELS: I saw you.

AGNES: Well...It is a free country.

DOCTOR TITTELS: In Germany men don't give their wives forty dollars to get drunk in the middle of the day.

AGNES: No?

DOCTOR TITTELS: Never.

AGNES: I suppose you're right.

DOCTOR TITTELS: Of course I'm right—

AGNES: They would give them marks.

DOCTOR TITTELS: Disgraceful.

(DOCTOR TITTELS searches for his papers as AGNES stumbles into the kitchen.)

DOCTOR TITTELS: I don't know how I'm supposed to find anything in this stupid house. Pig sty. Drunkard housewife.

AGNES: *(O S)* Shall I make meat loaf for dinner?

DOCTOR TITTELS: I don't care!

AGNES: *(O S)* Meatballs it is! *(She enters with Chapter Five in her hands. It's frozen together.)*

AGNES: You might want to defrost before serving, dear.

DOCTOR TITTELS: What happened?

AGNES: "The Frigid Woman" helped herself to the ice cream...your favorite flavor—

DOCTOR TITTELS: You did this.

AGNES: Did I?

DOCTOR TITTELS: Of course.

AGNES: Aren't I clever.

DOCTOR TITTELS: I should have never left my practice.

AGNES: I agree, dear.

DOCTOR TITTELS: It's chaos here. Chaos all the time. A man can't think in this den of domesticity—

AGNES: Hungry?

DOCTOR TITTELS: Yes.

AGNES: Well, good. Dinner will be ready in four hours.

DOCTOR TITTELS: Four hours?

(AGNES *lies down on the couch.*)

AGNES: Get to work then. You've got a deadline to meet. (*She passes out.*)

(*On the video screen,* JOY *takes out two bottles of beer.*)

DAN: *(O S)* Were you a virgin when you got married?

(JOY *looks at* DAN *and smiles, as she responds to his smile.*)

DAN: *(O S)* No. How old were you? The first time—

JOY: How old were you?

DAN: *(O S)* Again...we're not talking about me—

JOY: Sixteen? ...Seventeen?

(*Silence*)

DAN: *(O S)* I'm trying to be objective here. (*He sneezes O S.*)

JOY: Bless you. Good luck with that.

DAN: *(O S)* Thank you. Because I'm a man? ...You think a man can't make an honest study of women's sexuality.

JOY: I think all conversations about sex are only relative to what anyone *is willing* to tell you—man or woman—

DAN: *(O S)* I don't—

JOY: You're a perfect example.

DAN: *(O S)* I'm not the example— (*He sneezes again, O S.*) Do you have a cat?

JOY: Because I'm a single woman, I have a cat?

DAN: *(O S)* No. I'm allergic—

JOY: You know, I could tell you I jack off twice a day or have never had an orgasm in my life or that I worked as a prostitute for ten years in a Nevada whorehouse and

would you really know anymore about me? I don't
have a cat.

DAN: *(O S)* I'm really not trying to get to know you.
I'm just trying to learn more about your relationship
to sex—

JOY: Oh. You can separate the two?

(Long sigh O S)

DAN: *(O S)* I was eighteen. The first time I had sex.
She was seventeen. O K? Now you.

JOY: Fifteen.

DAN: *(O S)* Fifteen? Seems young... Did you worry
about consequences? Pregnancy? AIDS, S T Ds, Love?

JOY: Love is a consequence?

DAN: *(O S)* Isn't it?

JOY: Huh. Did you? ...Worry?

DAN: *(O S)* It was the eighties. The height of AIDS.

JOY: Right... Well, we didn't worry about that. Not one
bit. That was a freedom you guys missed...sex was just
what you did when you met someone new. It wasn't
such a big deal...you didn't have to talk yourself to
death before you jumped into bed with someone.

DAN: *(O S)* You think people talk too much about it
now, before they enter into a sexual relationship?

JOY: Ad nauseum.

DAN: *(O S)* You seem to like to talk.

JOY: I'm not trying to sleep with you.

SCENE FOUR:
THE FRIGID WOMAN

(DOCTOR TITTELS sits behind the typewriter, with a serious case of writer's block. He can't think of one thing to type, and when he does, it's the wrong letter.)

AGNES: What time is it?

(DOCTOR TITTELS stares at the typewriter.)

AGNES: Fritz?

(DOCTOR TITTELS continues to try and work.)

AGNES: What time is it?

DOCTOR TITTELS: Is the hobo awake now?

AGNES: Is it late?

DOCTOR TITTELS: If you call nine o'clock late, I suppose it is. Late.

AGNES: Oh my. *(She slowly stands.)*

DOCTOR TITTELS: I don't know how I'm supposed to work on an empty stomach.

AGNES: I'm on my way to the kitchen.

DOCTOR TITTELS: It's hard to concentrate when I'm hungry.

AGNES: I know, Fritz.

(DOCTOR TITTELS returns to his typewriter.)

DOCTOR TITTELS: I wish I could sleep all day. Lounge to all hours. Nothing to bother me. Not a care in the world.

(AGNES offers DOCTOR TITTELS the bottle of scotch.)

AGNES: Cocktail?

(DOCTOR TITTELS studies the bottle.)

DOCTOR TITTELS: I don't have a glass.

(AGNES *returns with a glass. She fills it and sets it on* DOCTOR TITTELS's *desk.*)

DOCTOR TITTELS: Are we out of ice?

(AGNES *enters the kitchen and returns with a tray of ice. Drops the ice in the glass.*)

DOCTOR TITTELS: Nuts would be nice.

(AGNES *exits into the kitchen and returns with a bowl of nuts. Sets them on* DOCTOR TITTELS's *desk.*)

DOCTOR TITTELS: Did you have a nice lunch?

AGNES: Yes.

DOCTOR TITTELS: Your sister alright?

AGNES: Fine.

DOCTOR TITTELS: What did you talk about?

AGNES: The usual—

DOCTOR TITTELS: Is she coming for your birthday?

AGNES: No, she can't—

DOCTOR TITTELS: Did she ask about the book?

AGNES: Not really.

(AGNES *tries to exit into the kitchen again,* DOCTOR TITTELS *follows, stops her.*)

DOCTOR TITTELS: Please. I know how you two gossip.

AGNES: It never came up.

DOCTOR TITTELS: Never?

AGNES: No.

DOCTOR TITTELS: Why not?

AGNES: It just didn't.

DOCTOR TITTELS: What did you talk about?

AGNES: I told you. The usual things.

DOCTOR TITTELS: What "usual things"? Aren't I part of the "usual things"?

AGNES: Not always, dear—

(AGNES *tries to go into the kitchen again.* DOCTOR TITTELS *stops her.*)

DOCTOR TITTELS: You told her, didn't you.

AGNES: How am I to cook dinner, if you keep—

DOCTOR TITTELS: You told her it was late, didn't you.

AGNES: No.

DOCTOR TITTELS: Of course you did. You couldn't help it. You like to see me fail, don't you?

AGNES: Why would I do that, dear—

DOCTOR TITTELS: This book, this book could change the way women think about themselves, Agnes. The way men think of women. The way medical professionals deal with the sexual elements of a woman's psyche. Do you know how much pressure that is?

AGNES: I would think it is a lot of pressure, dear.

DOCTOR TITTELS: I am trying to capture the most intimate details of women and put it to paper.

AGNES: Yes you are, dear—

DOCTOR TITTELS: I could be the laughing stock!

(DOCTOR TITTELS *paces back to his desk.* AGNES *follows.*)

AGNES: Who would laugh at you?

DOCTOR TITTELS: Oh, they all would! They'd all love to see Fritz Tittels fail! Make a mockery of my successful career—

AGNES: Why?

DOCTOR TITTELS: They're jealous!

AGNES: You need to eat something—

DOCTOR TITTELS: You make your success out of, out of this, a taboo subject, in this country, Agnes, and they are like jackals coming in for the kill. 'How dare this German write about our bedrooms!' 'How dare he air our public shame!' 'We Americans can't have sex, we go to church on Sunday!'

AGNES: Fritz—

DOCTOR TITTELS: 'Our women don't want orgasms, they want kitchenware!'

AGNES: Now—

DOCTOR TITTELS: 'Just put a new hat on her and she's happy.'

AGNES: You exaggerate.

DOCTOR TITTELS: Do I?

AGNES: Yes.

DOCTOR TITTELS: You don't know what kind of pressure I'm under. No. You don't know at all.

(AGNES *takes a seat.*)

AGNES: I think you're making excuses.

DOCTOR TITTELS: What?

AGNES: I do.

DOCTOR TITTELS: I thought you were going to cook dinner.

AGNES: I think you are afraid of this book.

(DOCTOR TITTELS *pours himself another drink.*)

DOCTOR TITTELS: You think so?

AGNES: Yes.

(DOCTOR TITTELS *mumbles something in German.*)

(AGNES *waits.*)

DOCTOR TITTELS: Of course I'm afraid of it! I'm, I'm pulling down the, the underpants of American women! In public! I'm taking off their brassieres, and hanging them out for all to see!

AGNES: So—

DOCTOR TITTELS: So?

AGNES: Do it well, dear, and get on with it.

(DOCTOR TITTELS *mumbles more German.*)

AGNES: I don't speak German.

DOCTOR TITTELS: You don't understand.

AGNES: Have you forgotten, Fritz, that my underpants are included in those you are hanging out to dry?

DOCTOR TITTELS: Of course not—

AGNES: That I am *Mrs* Fritz Tittels?

DOCTOR TITTELS: Of course not—

AGNES: That I stand more naked than any other woman inside the pages of your book?

DOCTOR TITTELS: Of course not—

AGNES: Then you understand that I want you to write the best damn sex book anyone has ever laid eyes on—

DOCTOR TITTELS: Well—

AGNES: That *The Sex Habits of American Women* be a best-seller because you have not been afraid to reveal the secrets of the woman you know best—

DOCTOR TITTELS: Agnes—

AGNES: And the wife that has no patience for your fears.

DOCTOR TITTELS: Agnes—

AGNES: We both know you like success too much to be bothered with failure.

DOCTOR TITTELS: You're right.

AGNES: Of course I'm right. Now... *(She heads for the kitchen.)* If you'll let me get to that dinner—

DOCTOR TITTELS: Agnes.

AGNES: Yes, dear?

DOCTOR TITTELS: I love you.

AGNES: I know.

(AGNES exits into the kitchen. DOCTOR TITTELS gathers his papers from the floor.)

(JOY is standing straight up, turns around, as if she is a model, to show her entire self. The camera is moving backward, as DAN speaks.)

DAN: O.S. *(Whispers)* Exhibit A. Caucasian. Roughly forty-five to fifty years old. Joy Lawrence— *(He trips, O S.)*

(We see shots of the wall, ceiling, etc.)

DAN: *(O S)* Shit.

(More views of the floor and room as DAN gets his balance.)

JOY: *(O S)* Are you O K?

DAN: *(O S)* Yeah...yeah. Fine.

SCENE FIVE:
THE BEDROOM

(Two twin beds. AGNES and DOCTOR TITTELS lie in one bed together.)

(He wipes his forehead and she adjusts her hair as he climbs out of her bed, and into his own.)

DOCTOR TITTELS: Good night.

AGNES: Night, dear.

(AGNES lies awake, but soon, DOCTOR TITTELS is snoring.)

(The blankets can be seen slightly moving in her bed, as AGNES touches herself.)

(She lets out a soft moan as she climaxes.)

(The blankets, and AGNES, lie very still.)

(On the video screen, JOY stands showing the scars on her body.)

JOY: That's where I fell out of a car. They had to reinflate my lung...kind of like a beach ball... here's where an old boyfriend and I got a little too "interested" in some "alternative" bedroom activities...*that* hurt. I decided to give the whip back to the horse after that...here's where my daughter came into the world...feet first...and here...well... here's where...god, I can't believe I'm showing you this...you better get that deal with P B S or I'll be very disappointed, Dan... *(She laughs...lifts her shirt higher)* This is where they took my left breast...

(JOY's smiling face changes, looking at the cameraman/ interviewer. The video grows blurry, out of focus.)

JOY: Oh, sweetheart... *(She laughs, reaches toward the camera)* You don't...you don't have to cry...I'm used to it now.

SCENE SIX:
AGE

(The stage is dark and AGNES *sits at the table with her eyes closed. She is wearing a birthday hat.)*

*(*DAISY *enters from the kitchen with a cake and lit candles.* DOCTOR TITTELS *follows, and they too wear hats. They sing.)*

DAISY & DOCTOR TITTELS:
Happy Birthday...dear Mom/Agnes...
Happy Birthday to you.

DAISY: And many more...

*(*AGNES *makes a wish and blows out the candles.)*

DOCTOR TITTELS: Get the lights, Daisy.

(They sit in the dark.)

DAISY: You get the lights.

DOCTOR TITTELS: Just do as you're told.

DAISY: I'm not a child.

(Finally AGNES *gets up and turns on the lights.)*

AGNES: Who wants cake?

DAISY: I do!

DOCTOR TITTELS: Big piece for me!

AGNES: I need a knife.

DOCTOR TITTELS: You forgot the knife, Daisy.

DAISY: You forgot it—

DOCTOR TITTELS: It's your mother's birthday, just go get—

DAISY: Stop telling me what to do.

DOCTOR TITTELS: You stop telling me what to do.

(AGNES exits into the kitchen, returns with a knife and plates.)

AGNES: Cake for everyone.

DAISY: I baked it myself.

AGNES: Beautiful. *(She cuts the cake.)* So many candles. Looks like—

DAISY: Seven. One for every ten years.

AGNES: That would be seventy, dear.

DOCTOR TITTELS: Your mother is sixty-six.

AGNES: Sixty-five.

(AGNES cuts and hands them each a piece.)

DOCTOR TITTELS: There's too much frosting on the cake.

DAISY: I thought you were seventy, Mom.

DOCTOR TITTELS: Where's the cake?

DAISY: Don't eat it, Daddy.

DOCTOR TITTELS: I just don't understand why there's an inch of frosting on here.

DAISY: Mom likes it that way, don't you, Mom?

AGNES: I don't like frosting, dear.

(The cake is terrible, but they all try and eat it.)

AGNES: But this, this is delicious.

(The doorbell rings O S.)

DOCTOR TITTELS: That must be Edgar.

AGNES: You invited Edgar?

DOCTOR TITTELS: Of course. He wants to hear the progress on my book.

AGNES: Wonderful.

(DOCTOR TITTELS *exits.*)

DAISY: Are you sure you're not seventy, Mom?

AGNES: Yes, dear.

DAISY: You're sure—

AGNES: I still have my memory, Daisy.

(EDGAR *enters with* DOCTOR TITTELS.)

DOCTOR TITTELS: Here he is! Welcome, welcome.

AGNES: What a lovely surprise.

EDGAR: Happy Birthday, Mrs Tittels.

AGNES: Oh, who told you...

EDGAR: Doctor Tittels mentioned it.

(EDGAR *hands* AGNES *a small box.*)

AGNES: You shouldn't have.

EDGAR: I did.

AGNES: Look at that.

(*A broach is inside.*)

AGNES: Oh Edgar. How beautiful.

EDGAR: It's just a little something I saw in the store. Very Alexander Calder, don't you think?

AGNES: Oh, yes.

DAISY: Daddy didn't even get her something that nice.

DOCTOR TITTELS: That television was very expensive.

DAISY: You bought that for yourself. Mother has no interest in it—

AGNES: I love them both. Thank you. I'm spoiled. *(She pins it on her dress.)*

EDGAR: Daisy.

DAISY: Edgar.

EDGAR: How are you?

DAISY: Depressed. You?

EDGAR: Well, thank you. Very well. Are you in therapy—

DAISY: I need another shrink in my life like a deer needs a gun.

EDGAR: What?

DAISY: Skip it.

AGNES: Would you like some cake, Edgar?

EDGAR: Oh. Yes. Please—

DAISY: I baked it myself—

DOCTOR TITTELS: Brave man.

(EDGAR takes a bite.)

EDGAR: Hmm. Wow. That's a lot of frosting.

AGNES: Who wants coffee? *(She exits into the kitchen.)*

EDGAR: Everyone at the office sends their regards, Doctor Tittels.

DOCTOR TITTELS: Thank you. My old office still empty?

EDGAR: No. No. Hasn't been for some time.

DOCTOR TITTELS: Oh.

EDGAR: Dr. Stiles has it now. She's very good. Very good indeed. From Radcliffe, I think.

DOCTOR TITTELS: A woman? Impressive.

EDGAR: Yes.

DOCTOR TITTELS: Did you hear that, Daisy?

DAISY: Loud and clear.

DOCTOR TITTELS: A woman.

EDGAR: Finally thinking of leaving your calling to
the public schools to follow in your father's footsteps,
Daisy?

DAISY: No.

EDGAR: Oh.

DOCTOR TITTELS: Daisy insists on walking in sand.
Her footsteps will be washed away and forgotten.

DAISY: *(Mocking gaiety)* "Like a bird."

(Silence)

EDGAR: So. Doctor Tittels. Without further ado.
How's the book coming?

DOCTOR TITTELS: Fantastic.

EDGAR: I've been hearing whispers all around about it.

DOCTOR TITTELS: You have?

EDGAR: Yes, sir.

DOCTOR TITTELS: What kind?

EDGAR: Enthusiastic anticipation.

DOCTOR TITTELS: Huh.

EDGAR: Is there a problem sir?

DOCTOR TITTELS: No, no. Heavens no. Drink, Edgar?

EDGAR: No, thank you, sir.

DOCTOR TITTELS: Would you like to hear a chapter or
two? I'd welcome your opinion.

EDGAR: My opinion, sir?

DOCTOR TITTELS: Of course.

EDGAR: I'd be honored.

DOCTOR TITTELS: Well then. Grab a seat here and—

DAISY: Are you gonna read it out loud?

DOCTOR TITTELS: Why?

DAISY: "The recent studies of sexual practices among women in their thirties and forties report that the desire for fornication is increased into a near heated frenzy. Women admit the desire becomes so fierce that they must resort to rubbing up against table legs and taking extra long subway rides just to get closer to the hard pole pressed against their—"

DOCTOR TITTELS: You don't have to listen, Daisy.

(EDGAR *laughs.*)

EDGAR: I'd read that.

DOCTOR TITTELS: She's making that up.

DAISY: You think Mom wants to listen to it, day after day?

DOCTOR TITTELS: She is a captive audience—

DAISY: For Christ's sake. It's her birthday. Let's listen to some music or something. Something real. *(She turns on the radio.)*

DOCTOR TITTELS: Turn that noise off—

(AGNES *enters with a tray and coffee pot.*)

AGNES: Oh, doesn't that sound lovely. I just love music in the house.

(DAISY *turns it up.*)

AGNES: Makes me want to dance.

(DAISY *takes the tray and sets it down. Takes* AGNES *in her arms and dances with her.*)

AGNES: My goodness. You're a fine dancer, Daisy.

DAISY: Am I?

AGNES: Look how you just take the lead.

(*They dance around the living room.*)

AGNES: Oh, what fun. This is a swell present. Oh my...

(*The men watch.*)

AGNES: Aren't you boys going to cut in?

(EDGAR *begins*—)

DOCTOR TITTELS: No.

DAISY: Daddy doesn't believe in dancing. He might just lose control and enjoy himself.

AGNES: He danced at our wedding.

DAISY: Did you, Daddy?

DOCTOR TITTELS: Of course I did.

DAISY: I don't believe you. I don't think you're capable of fun.

(DOCTOR TITTELS *sets down his drink.*)

(*He walks over and waits for* DAISY *to step aside.*)

DAISY: What?

DOCTOR TITTELS: Move.

DAISY: What's the magic word?

(DOCTOR TITTELS *mumbles in German.*)

DAISY: It's Mom's birthday—

DOCTOR TITTELS: Please.

DAISY: Nope.

DOCTOR TITTELS: Get out of the way—

DAISY: "May I cut in?"

(DOCTOR TITTELS *pushes* DAISY *aside.*)

(He awkwardly dances with AGNES.)

AGNES: Isn't this fun, Fritz?

DOCTOR TITTELS: Sure.

*(*EDGAR *and* DAISY *stand aside, watching. He smiles at her.)*

EDGAR: Shall we?

*(*EDGAR *and* DAISY *join in the dancing. There is no chemistry between them. They both keep trying to lead. He stops.)*

EDGAR: Shall I lead now?

DAISY: Sure. If you're man enough.

EDGAR: I've been told I am.

(They try again just as the song ends.)

EDGAR: Well.

AGNES: Oh, what a wonderful birthday. I could just dance for hours. For hours.

(A new song begins.)

AGNES: Listen to that—

*(*EDGAR *holds out his hand to* AGNES *to dance.)*

EDGAR: May I have the honor—

*(*DOCTOR TITTELS *turns off the radio.)*

DOCTOR TITTELS: It's too loud.

DAISY: Daddy. Mother was dancing—

DOCTOR TITTELS: It's hard on the carpet.

AGNES: Well—

DAISY: Please.

DOCTOR TITTELS: Edgar didn't come all the way over here for frivolous activity—

EDGAR: I don't mind—

AGNES: Just one more—

DAISY: It's Mother's birthday—

DOCTOR TITTELS: Time is of the essence—

AGNES: But—

DOCTOR TITTELS: I'm on a deadline—

DAISY: No one should have too much fun, right Daddy? *(She exits.)*

DOCTOR TITTELS: Here, Edgar. Let me show you my masterpiece.

(DOCTOR TITTELS shuttles EDGAR off stage, to his office.)

(AGNES is left alone, still inclined to dance.)

AGNES: Well then...

(AGNES straightens her dress; the music now gone from the room.)

AGNES: I guess I'll clean the kitchen. *(She exits into the kitchen.)*

SCENE SEVEN

(Night)

(AGNES sits alone in the living room, close to the radio, listening. Bing Crosby sings Where the Blue of the Night [Meets the Gold of the Day].*)*

(On the video screen. JOY *sits on the couch. The camera moves in closer, as she thinks.)*

JOY: You know...I used to think that good sex and love always worked well together...but I'm not sure of that now.... Seems they often miss each other...like oil and vinegar...always put together to make something taste better...they are good at floating beside or near each other...but never really completely...mixing....

SCENE EIGHT:
FLAVOR

(Restaurant. AGNES *sits alone, looking over a menu. She keeps looking up, waiting for someone to join. She checks her watch. She waits. She begins to stand to leave, then quickly sits again. Smiles)*

*(*EDGAR *enters smiling. He grabs* AGNES's *hand as he sits at the table and she blushes.)*

EDGAR: I'm late I'm late. So sorry I'm late. It couldn't be helped. I am sorry.

AGNES: Oh no, not to worry. I haven't been here long.

EDGAR: My patient decided to talk today. I've spent a year working with this woman and today, BAM! The flood gates opened. I mean, today, she—well, you know I can't go into details, of course, it's all extremely confidential, you know that, but—she, □ wow, she discovered the *one* thing that made her happy. One simple thing. Outside of everything else in her complicated life, she found the one thing that made her, just her, purely happy.

AGNES: What was it?

EDGAR: I can't tell you. I'm sorry.

AGNES: Of course. Of course.

EDGAR: But, whew...it was amazing. I am so happy for her. We were both crying. Oh... Huh... You think she'll still respect me now?

AGNES: I don't know...I'm sure she—

EDGAR: It was just so poignant. And intimate... Watching her find something so Truthful inside herself. I couldn't stop myself...of course she'll respect me—but

I won't let it happen again. I just—Can you believe it?
Wow. Very exciting stuff. I'm sorry. I'm very excited.
(He takes a big breath. Claps his hands) I'm sorry. I'm just,
wow—

AGNES: I like it.

EDGAR: Do you?

AGNES: It's rather sweet.

EDGAR: Your husband would call me childish.

AGNES: My husband calls a child childish. A dog
dogish. A woman weak. And himself, brilliant. You
can't trust him.

EDGAR: He is a brilliant teacher.

(AGNES looks over the menu.)

AGNES: So I'm told.

EDGAR: You look lovely.

AGNES: Do I?

EDGAR: Put down that menu.

AGNES: Will you flatter me?

EDGAR: Yes.

(AGNES slowly sets down the menu.)

EDGAR: You could steal my heart in that color.

AGNES: Really?

EDGAR: Yes.

AGNES: Oh Edgar—

EDGAR: That blue is wasted on any other woman.

AGNES: Stop.

EDGAR: Even the ocean couldn't wear it like you.

AGNES: Please.

EDGAR: Or the sky.

(AGNES *fans herself with the menu.*)

EDGAR: The sky wouldn't know what to do with it at all. It would want to add passing clouds. Sunshine. Birds here and there. No, no. It's meant for you.

AGNES: Oh Edgar—

EDGAR: Nothing—wait—Picasso. Yes, Picasso might be the only one I would let touch that blue. Yes. He understands it. He spent years in that color. Searching. Yes... He knew what it could do.

AGNES: Oh—

EDGAR: Only he could do it justice. Outside of you, of course.

AGNES: You are too much. Really.

EDGAR: I am so excited, Agnes. A real breakthrough. I can't tell you how excited I am.

AGNES: You're telling me now.

EDGAR: I guess I am. Wow. Let's celebrate. Champagne? Shall we have champagne? Yes, yes. We must. I insist. The best in the house. And I must call my father and my brother and Doctor Tittels right away to tell them—

AGNES: Doctor Tittels will be proud.

EDGAR: He will, won't he?

AGNES: Of course.

EDGAR: Where's the waiter? Have you seen the waiter?

AGNES: He's over there somewhere—

EDGAR: Agnes, tell me something.

AGNES: I'll try—

EDGAR: Do you think I'm brilliant?

AGNES: Oh, Edgar...

EDGAR: I'm serious.

AGNES: It's a silly question.

EDGAR: Yes, but I need to know.

AGNES: Of course you are.

EDGAR: Really? When you think of me, do you think, Edgar Green..."brilliant"?

AGNES: I think many things when I think of you.

EDGAR: You do?

AGNES: Yes.

EDGAR: Like what?

AGNES: Edgar.

EDGAR: Yes.

AGNES: Can I tell you a secret?

EDGAR: Please. Oh yes. Please. Anything. Sure. I'm good at secrets. Please. Yes—

AGNES: I've been stroking my husband's ego for forty-seven years.

EDGAR: Forty-seven years—

AGNES: That's a long time, isn't it?

EDGAR: Yes. Yes. Very long. Wow. Almost fifty—

AGNES: Yes, almost fifty years. And when I met you, with all your boyish charm and wild enthusiasm, I was intoxicated.

EDGAR: Intoxicated—

AGNES: You made me feel free of such things. I feel eighteen again, and you know, I never really did feel eighteen when I was eighteen.

EDGAR: Yes—

AGNES: And then we started meeting like this...

(They both smile coyly.)

AGNES: And the things we've...shared... *(She smiles. Fans herself with the menu again)* But...you know what I've grown to treasure most?

EDGAR: Treasure? What a marvelous word...What? *(He drinks his whole glass of water at one time.)* I'm sorry, continue. I'm very excited—

AGNES: I treasure that you choose to sit across the table from a sixty-five year old woman and tell her she is more beautiful than the sky—

EDGAR: Oh yes. Head above heels more beautiful—

AGNES: And that I am that woman.

EDGAR: Yes you are—

AGNES: I am that woman, Edgar.

EDGAR: Oh. Yes. Indeed.

AGNES: Let me be her.

(AGNES smiles. Briefly touches EDGAR's hand.)

EDGAR: Right. Yes. Agnes. I'm sorry. I understand. I do. I understand—

AGNES: Now. How about that champagne?

EDGAR: The champagne. The champagne! Yes. Oh, by all means. Waiter?

(On the video screen, JOY continues.)

DAN: *(O S)* Do you ever get lonely?

JOY: Yes.

DAN: *(O S)* What makes you feel lonely?

JOY: Besides being alone?

DAN: *(O S)* Well, is it the sex or love that you miss?

JOY: thinks about it, begins to answer, but stops, unsure.

SCENE NINE

(The living room)

(DOCTOR TITTLES sits on the couch, papers everywhere.)

(AGNES enters with a bag of groceries, singing.)

DOCTOR TITTELS: Nice lunch?

AGNES: Wonderful.

DOCTOR TITTELS: How's your sister?

AGNES: Wonderful.

DOCTOR TITTELS: The weather?

AGNES: Wonderful.

DOCTOR TITTELS: It's cloudy.

AGNES: Is it? *(Still singing, she exits into the kitchen and returns, refills a candy dish.)*

DOCTOR TITTELS: Agnes.

AGNES: Yes, dear?

(DOCTOR TITTLES gives AGNES a look and she stops singing.)

(She whistles instead. He looks at her again. She smiles.)

DOCTOR TITTELS: Daisy called.

AGNES: Did she?

DOCTOR TITTELS: She's coming over.

AGNES: Oh?

DOCTOR TITTELS: So she says.

AGNES: Alone?

DOCTOR TITTELS: No.

AGNES: Who's she bringing?

DOCTOR TITTELS: I don't know—

AGNES: A man?

DOCTOR TITTELS: I don't know—

AGNES: Are they staying for dinner?

DOCTOR TITTELS: I didn't ask.

AGNES: Why not?

DOCTOR TITTELS: Because I'm stuck in SHIT'S CREEK WITHOUT A PADDLE, AGNES!

AGNES: No need to shout, dear.

(DOCTOR TITTLES *mumbles something in German, puts his head in his hands. Throws the papers off the desk.*)

DOCTOR TITTELS: The sex habits of American women...what was I thinking? ...I'm German!

AGNES: Fritz...

DOCTOR TITTELS: Every time I get my evidence in order, these charts...these endless charts...case studies... something subverts it. I swear, I don't know anything more about this book than when I started. Less!

AGNES: No—

DOCTOR TITTELS: Yes! From what I can tell, American women have more covert sex habits than, than you have shoes in the closet.

AGNES: I don't have a lot of shoes.

DOCTOR TITTELS: A pair for every dress.

AGNES: That's fashion, dear. Not excess.

DOCTOR TITTELS: Every time I think I'm finished, I find horrible ideas I'd forgotten about. Interviews. Women blindly searching for random sexual encounters...and, and happiness...sometimes love even isn't mentioned, Agnes...no...no...these things that just can't be true!

AGNES: Fritz—

DOCTOR TITTELS: My colleagues are smiling now, I'm sure of it.

AGNES: Let them smile—

DOCTOR TITTELS: Doctor Johannson, and Roberts, that smug Doctor Hughes? Enjoying every minute of it!

AGNES: Let them—

DOCTOR TITTELS: I told the publisher I'd have it done in two weeks!

AGNES: And you will.

DOCTOR TITTELS: That was two months ago!

AGNES: Fritz—

DOCTOR TITTELS: It's crap!

AGNES: It is not.

DOCTOR TITTELS: What if all women really want is mindless pleasure?!

AGNES: No. No. Fritz. It's very compelling. Just look here... *(She collects the papers from the floor. Grabs the first one she can and reads.)* "...No healthy, full-blooded American girl should be deviated from her pursuit of love, happiness and an active, fulfilling sex life." ...You see there?

(DOCTOR TITTLES nods, listening. AGNES continues.)

AGNES: "However, in some families, this pursuit is made more difficult for the daughter by her pathological parents."—

(DAISY barges in.)

DAISY: What's up, folks?

(*Her friend,* RUBY LAWRENCE, *enters behind her.*)

AGNES: Well, look who it is. My goodness. It's been forever. Little Ruby—

RUBY: Mrs Tittels. Mister Tittels.

(AGNES *hugs* RUBY.)

AGNES: Look at you. How beautiful you've become.

RUBY: Please.

AGNES: Marriage must agree with you.

RUBY: Oh yes.

AGNES: Daisy told us you bought a house last year.

RUBY: Yes, ma'am. You should come by.

AGNES: Your husband's well?

RUBY: He travels more with his promotion.

AGNES: And children?

DAISY: Mother.

AGNES: I can't ask about children?

(RUBY *steps back and reveals a tiny growing belly.*)

AGNES: My goodness. Congratulations. I guess you're not the little girl next door anymore, are you?

RUBY: I guess not.

AGNES: It's best to have children at your age. You know, I didn't get pregnant with Daisy until I was almost thirty—

DAISY: Mom!

(DAISY *and* AGNES *exchange a look.*)

RUBY: I'm redecorating my kitchen.

AGNES: Wonderful.

RUBY: Daisy's going to paint it for me.

AGNES: Isn't that nice.

RUBY: She fixed the sink today. And she's building shelves in my bedroom.

(DAISY *enters with a bottle of scotch and glasses.*)

AGNES: How thoughtful you are, Daisy.

RUBY: Isn't she?

DAISY: Who wants a drink?

DOCTOR TITTELS: Me.

RUBY: Mister Tittels. Daisy said you're working on a book.

DOCTOR TITTELS: Finished any day now.

RUBY: What's it about?

DOCTOR TITTELS: The sex habits of American women.

RUBY: Sounds racy.

DOCTOR TITTELS: Psychological.

RUBY: I see.

DAISY: Daddy thinks he's the next Freud.

RUBY: Who's that?

(DAISY *laughs, toasts* RUBY, *hands her a drink.*)

DAISY: I love you, Ruby.

RUBY: What?

DOCTOR TITTELS: Doctor Freud was a genius of a man—

DAISY: Crackpot shrink. Keep clear of him.

DOCTOR TITTELS: She doesn't know what she's talking about.

DAISY: What's for dinner, Mom?

AGNES: I don't know.

DOCTOR TITTELS: Your mother and her sister have taken to lazying their days away like a couple of hobos. She comes home drunk, singing, and carefree.

DAISY: Mother how could you?

AGNES: What?

DAISY: Enjoy yourself like that.

AGNES: It's lunch—

DAISY: And Daddy has to stay home all day thinking about naked women having orgasms.

RUBY: Oh my—

DOCTOR TITTELS: That's enough—

DAISY: Oh, you can say it all in our house now, Ruby. Orgasm. Vagina. Penis. *Ménage à trois.*

RUBY: What's that?

DAISY: What?

RUBY: *Ménage à*—

DAISY: When three people sleep together.

RUBY: Three?!

DAISY: Yes.

AGNES: I'm going to start dinner. *(She exits to the kitchen.)*

RUBY: How could three people do that—

DAISY: Ask Daddy. He's the expert.

DOCTOR TITTELS: Daisy is just trying to embarrass me.

RUBY: I'm going to help Mrs Tittels with dinner—

DOCTOR TITTELS: No, no. Let me show you my book.

RUBY: Oh, Mister Tittels, I don't know much about those things.

DOCTOR TITTELS: You must know something, Ruby?

RUBY: No, really—

DOCTOR TITTELS: You're pregnant—

RUBY: I'm going to help Mrs Tittels. *(She quickly exits into the kitchen.)*

(DAISY sits on the couch, drinking. Staring at her father.)

(DOCTOR TITTELS tries to work.)

DOCTOR TITTELS: What?

DAISY: If you know so much about sex, Doctor Tittels, why'd it take Mom twelve years to get pregnant?

DOCTOR TITTELS: They are two different things.

DAISY: Still...

(DOCTOR TITTELS waits.)

DOCTOR TITTELS: Still what?

DAISY: You must have been doing something wrong.

DOCTOR TITTELS: Sometimes I wish I had never done it "right"—

DAISY: All those years...I imagine there were some whispers among your friends. Colleagues.

DOCTOR TITTELS: I wouldn't know.

DAISY: Some doubts about yourself as a man.

DOCTOR TITTELS: No.

DAISY: Some doubts in Mom about your...you know...

DOCTOR TITTELS: Never.

DAISY: Manhood?

DOCTOR TITTELS: You weren't the first pregnancy.

DAISY: What?

DOCTOR TITTELS: Nothing.

DAISY: Daddy?

DOCTOR TITTELS: Never mind.

(DAISY *hovers over* DOCTOR TITTLES*'s desk.*)

DAISY: What do you mean?

DOCTOR TITTELS: Nothing. Go sit down. You make me nervous.

(DAISY *sits on his papers.*)

DOCTOR TITTELS: Always you must make me crazy. Since you were little. Like a snap turtle—

(DAISY *threatens to pour her drink on* DOCTOR TITTLES*'s papers.*)

DOCTOR TITTELS: There, there was "activity" before you. It just...they just didn't survive—

DAISY: How many—

DOCTOR TITTELS: That's not important. And don't you ask your mother—

DAISY: Mom?

(DOCTOR TITTLES *slaps his hand over* DAISY*'s mouth.*)

DOCTOR TITTELS: You are a cruel girl.

(DAISY *shrugs,* DOCTOR TITTLES*'s hand still on her mouth.*)

DOCTOR TITTELS: There were three. Now leave it at that.

(DOCTOR TITTLES *takes his hand from* DAISY*'s mouth.*

DAISY: Your hands are clammy—

DOCTOR TITTELS: I mean it, Daisy—

DAISY: What happened?

DOCTOR TITTELS: They just didn't take. Leave it at that—

(AGNES *enters with a tray of cocktail wieners and gherkins, offering them.*)

AGNES: Wieners and pickles anyone? Ruby is in there making us her tuna casserole. How do you like that? Apparently she makes six of them a week. They are easy. I'm sure I made plenty of those when we first married, right Fritz?

DOCTOR TITTELS: You shouldn't mix fish and cheese.

DAISY: Why not?

DOCTOR TITTELS: When would a fish ever meet a cow? Would a fish visit the prairie? Would a cow go to the sea?

DAISY: They might meet at a party. A company mixer.

DOCTOR TITTELS: Only in America.

AGNES: Ruby is a sweet girl and we will all enjoy it thoroughly.

DOCTOR TITTELS: Couldn't be worse than Daisy's cooking.

AGNES: It's just so nice to have a pregnant girl in the house. So tender...the growing possibilities...the dreams...may be the closest I ever get to grandchildren.

DOCTOR TITTELS: Indeed.

AGNES: Look at Ruby. She's happy as a clam. She met her husband at church. You could go to church.

DAISY: Thank you, no.

AGNES: It might do you good.

DAISY: It makes me nauseous.

AGNES: Don't be silly.

DAISY: I vomit every time I enter a church.

AGNES: You exaggerate.

DAISY: Remember that time I puked in the offering tray?

AGNES: You were six.

DAISY: It was the beginning. Just the smell of the bibles makes me heave.

AGNES: You exaggerate.

DOCTOR TITTELS: Daisy's not going to find a husband until she gets in therapy. She needs professional help.

DAISY: I was raised by a "professional"—

DOCTOR TITTELS: You obviously have resentment towards your mother and me and I think it's just a matter of time before—

DAISY: I don't believe in your mind crap sex starved head banging Freud friendly theories. I never have, and I never will. Save it for your soon-to-be-forgotten book. I'm going to help Ruby.

DOCTOR TITTELS: It could change your life.

DAISY: Maybe you should have thought of that when I was a kid. Tried hugging me now and then. *(She exits into the kitchen.)*

(AGNES and DOCTOR TITTELS sit with their drinks, silent.)

DOCTOR TITTELS: I hugged her, didn't I?

AGNES: Of course you did.

DOCTOR TITTELS: Of course. *(Silence)* You're sure?

(Silence)

AGNES: You were very busy.

(On the video screen. In JOY's bedroom. She folds laundry on the bed.)

DAN: *(O S)* Did you come from a happy home?

JOY: Yes. And I'm not in denial. It really was.

DAN: *(O S)* Your parents had a good relationship, good marriage?

JOY: They had a great marriage. Still do. But, of course, I think it's because my mother made a lot of sacrifices.

DAN: *(O S)* Like what?

JOY: She didn't work, outside the house. My father and I were her life. She never looked for anything more—

DAN: *(O S)* More what?—

KATIE: *(O S)* When's dinner, Mom?

JOY: I don't know, sweetheart.

KATIE: *(O S)* I'm hungry. *(A frustrated* KATIE *has joined* JOY *on the bed.)* Moooommmm...I'm hungry.

JOY: You know where the kitchen is.

KATIE: Mom...I'm starving.... Can't he turn that camera off?

JOY: He's asking about sex, Katie...aren't you the new expert? Katie storms off.

KATIE: *(O S)* I hate you.

JOY: Where are you going? ...Hey...?

KATIE: *(O S)* Kelly's house.

JOY: Why?

KATIE: *(O S)* Her mother still feeds her.

SCENE TEN:
EXPANSION

(Lights up on AGNES *in* EDGAR's *arms in his bed. Low light from a window)*

AGNES: No?

EDGAR: Not really.

AGNES: You just say those kinds of things to make me feel better about myself.

EDGAR: I don't—

AGNES: I think you do.

EDGAR: I say what I feel is true.

*(*AGNES *plays with* EDGAR's *hair.)*

AGNES: Fritz wanted many.

EDGAR: I don't—

AGNES: Someday you'll meet a woman. Your age. Who makes you happy. She may want children.

EDGAR: I'm happy now.

*(*AGNES *settles in his arms. Suddenly coy)*

AGNES: Are you, Edgar?

EDGAR: Completely.

AGNES: Oh, my dear Prince.

EDGAR: I don't want a woman my age—

AGNES: You're a kind man—

EDGAR: I love you.

(Silence)

AGNES: Don't just flatter me with those words, Edgar.

EDGAR: I'm not. I don't. I do love you—

AGNES: Oh. Dear.

EDGAR: What?

(AGNES *sits up*.)

EDGAR: What's the matter?

AGNES: I feel nauseous.

EDGAR: Do you need some water?

AGNES: No. No.

EDGAR: I didn't mean to upset you.

AGNES: Heavens. I'm sweating—

EDGAR: I'm sorry—

AGNES: No. You didn't—I just—

EDGAR: What?

AGNES: I just...oh mercy—

EDGAR: Agnes, I'm sorry if my honesty is, is upsetting, but my feelings for you have been so, so, wonderful, and, and I just, I've, I've wanted to tell you that for sometime—

AGNES: I don't know what to do with that, Edgar.

EDGAR: What?

AGNES: *That.*

EDGAR: What?

AGNES: Those lovely words.

EDGAR: Yes?

AGNES: Where do I put them?

EDGAR: Put them?

AGNES: Your feelings for me. My feelings—I wasn't expecting this—my, there's just—

EDGAR: What?

AGNES: There's so many of them.

EDGAR: Aren't they wonderful.

AGNES: No.

(Silence)

EDGAR: No?

AGNES: I don't know where to put them, Edgar.
(She adjusts the sheets around her.) I just don't know.

EDGAR: Well, do you have to put them somewhere?

AGNES: Yes. *(She adjusts her hair. Her necklace)*

EDGAR: Can't you just feel them?

AGNES: No.

EDGAR: Why not?

AGNES: I can't.

EDGAR: Why not?

AGNES: Because I can't hold them. Not all of them.

EDGAR: You can try—

AGNES: No. I don't think so. Not without spilling out.
Ripping something. Mess. *(She stands. Begins pacing)*

EDGAR: Agnes please—

AGNES: Did, did you know that the first time I got
pregnant and, and lost it, Fritz fished the blood,
the fetus, from the toilet, sat on the bathroom floor,
and, and sobbed with it in his hands?

(EDGAR doesn't know how to respond.)

AGNES: Just sobbed.

EDGAR: Agnes—

AGNES: No one suspects him of such things.... He has a big heart, that man.

EDGAR: I know.

AGNES: I know every inch of him.

EDGAR: Of course.

AGNES: By rote.

EDGAR: Come here.

AGNES: But I'll never leave him.

EDGAR: I know.

AGNES: I'm too old for that.

EDGAR: I don't think so, by any means, but—

AGNES: You'll tire of me, Edgar.

EDGAR: Who says?

AGNES: Look at me.

EDGAR: I'm looking.

AGNES: My body is the body of an old woman.

EDGAR: And I want it.

AGNES: Parts of it move that never moved—

EDGAR: Who wants to stay still?

AGNES: My flesh escapes me—

EDGAR: Only if you let it—

AGNES: It blooms no more.

EDGAR: It's a garden. Look in the mirror—

AGNES: I shouldn't feel these things. For you. Not now. (*She sits on the end of the bed.*)

EDGAR: What?

AGNES: Bliss. (*She sighs hard.*) Hunger.

EDGAR: Come here—

AGNES: Nothing makes me happy anymore—

EDGAR: I'm sorry—

AGNES: I'm stretched out of myself, Edgar.

(EDGAR *moves closer to* AGNES.)

EDGAR: I'm sorry, but I love you, Agnes—

AGNES: I'm not sure where I'll fit again.

EDGAR: Don't worry.

(EDGAR *kisses* AGNES's *neck.*)

AGNES: And how?

(AGNES *lies down and reaches for* EDGAR.)

END OF ACT ONE

ACT TWO

(On the video screen, close-up on JOY's *face, looking at the camera confused.)*

JOY: What?

*(*JOY *smiles, responding to* DAN's *face O S.)*

JOY: Do I have a booger in my nose or something?

DAN: *(O S) (Laughing)* No...I want to sleep with you.

JOY: Really?

DAN: *(O S)* Yes.

JOY: But...wouldn't that compromise your "research",
Dan?

DAN: *(O S)* Yes.

SCENE ONE

(Six months later.)

(The living room)

*(*DOCTOR TITTLES, AGNES, DAISY, EDGAR *and* RUBY *enter through the door, happy and smiling.* RUBY *pushes a baby carriage, while* AGNES *holds the baby. They are all in nice party clothes.* DAISY *and* DOCTOR TITTLES *carry open bottles of champagne.)*

DOCTOR TITTELS: What a great success!

RUBY: I've never been to such a party.

AGNES: What a good baby she is, Ruby. Sleeping all the time. Don't you want to hold her, Daisy?

(DAISY *moves across the room.*)

EDGAR: You sure impressed them, Doctor Tittels.

DOCTOR TITTELS: Impressed them? I knocked their socks off.

EDGAR: It's an impressive book.

(DOCTOR TITTLES *holds a galley copy of his book up for inspection.*)

DOCTOR TITTELS: Impressive? It's groundbreaking.

EDGAR: Yes it is—

RUBY: I think you're famous, Doctor Tittels—

DOCTOR TITTELS: Who wants more champagne?

AGNES: I would, dear. Oh, let me get the glasses.

(AGNES *sets the baby in* DAISY's *hands and exits into the kitchen.*)

EDGAR: I'll help. (*He follows.*)

DOCTOR TITTELS: I am a happy man.

RUBY: I've never seen so many doctors in one room.

DOCTOR TITTELS: And they loved me.

(DAISY *quickly sets the baby in the carriage.*)

RUBY: So many glasses. They were all wearing glasses—

DOCTOR TITTELS: I swear, I saw envy in their eyes. And I loved it. What a success.

(DOCTOR TITTLES *begins to sing in German. Grabs* RUBY *to dance.*)

DAISY: Don't break something.

DOCTOR TITTELS: Can't your father be happy?

DAISY: It's a sex book. Not *War and Peace*.

DOCTOR TITTELS: Must you spoil everything?

RUBY: I thought it was wonderful.

DOCTOR TITTELS: Thank you, Ruby. You know what a father needs to hear.

RUBY: I didn't understand half the stuff people were talking about, but it was all so fancy, I didn't care.

DOCTOR TITTELS: First class.

DAISY: You paid for it.

DOCTOR TITTELS: I won't let you ruin my night—

(AGNES *enters with champagne glasses, and* EDGAR *follows with snacks.*)

AGNES: Here we are. (*She starts handing out glasses.*) Another toast to the great author.

DOCTOR TITTELS: That's me! I'm so happy...my family and friends here to share my joy...

(DOCTOR TITTLES *pours champagne into everyone's glasses.*)

RUBY: Mrs Tittels...your dress...you're coming undone—

AGNES: What dear?

RUBY: Your dress.

(AGNES' *dress is unbuttoned at the top.*)

AGNES: Oh my. Look at that. Must have been all the excitement—

EDGAR: A toast to Doctor Tittels...and his new book...and all his hard work—

DOCTOR TITTELS: There was hard work. Wasn't there? I worked very hard.

AGNES: You did, dear. You finally finished it—

DOCTOR TITTELS: I took a subject—and it is a difficult subject in this country, especially for women, don't let anyone tell you different—and I blew the lid off it and will blow the lids off women—and men—everywhere! Times are changing, and Fritz Tittels is at the forefront!

EDGAR: To changing times!

DOCTOR TITTELS: Indeed. *(He takes a large gulp. [He is beginning to grow more and more drunk.])* Did you see my colleagues? Did you hear them? Doctor Johannson? Hughes? Raves. Absolute raves! And their wives? Liberated! Captivated!

RUBY: The baby didn't cry once.

DOCTOR TITTELS: She was too captivated!

RUBY: Oh, you think she understood?—

DAISY: When she's sixteen she won't know why, but she'll suddenly feel so "liberated" she'll start growing her hair, going without a bra, and want to have wild sex across the country in the back of pick-up trucks and on the steering wheels of sports cars—

DOCTOR TITTELS: She might.

RUBY: Oh my.

DAISY: Dream on, Daddy.

RUBY: I don't know if I like that idea.

AGNES: I think it sounds fun.

DAISY: Mother, please.

AGNES: What?

DAISY: Let's go, Ruby. I've had enough. Imaginations are running wild here. Picturing my mother as a sweaty gypsy on the highway of life is my limit.

AGNES: Well, Daisy, women never thought they'd get the chance to vote, and look. What seemed impossible, became possible. Opportunities we thought we'd never have. When I was your age—

DAISY: Can it, Mom.

DOCTOR TITTELS: Daisy, don't speak to your mother—

DAISY: Just once I'd like to come into this house and not get a dissertation on some kind of psychological crotch problem or a lecture on 'when I was your age' or jab about my shriveling uterus because I'm not married and it embarrasses you to your friends.

AGNES: Who said that—

DAISY: I saw you talking behind my back, Mother—

AGNES: I'm free to talk, aren't I?

DAISY: And you, Daddy—

DOCTOR TITTELS: What'd I do?

DAISY: Shaking your head at me with all those four-eyed phonies. "She could have been so much more." More what? And maybe I don't want to be married. Ever think of that?

AGNES & DOCTOR TITTELS: No.

DOCTOR TITTELS: We weren't talking about you, Daisy. Really—

DAISY: We're never talking about me!

DOCTOR TITTELS: This is my night!

DAISY: It's always your night! Always you! Or Mother! Your friends! Your career. Get your coat, Ruby.

RUBY: Oh, O K—

AGNES: Don't spoil everything, Daisy. Sit down—

DAISY: I don't want to sit down, Mother. You can celebrate without me.

AGNES: We want you here—

DAISY: The old maid won't embarrass you anymore tonight. She's going home to her cats, her books, and her rotting bed.

AGNES: You don't embarrass us, dear. You're exaggerating—

DOCTOR TITTELS: This is my night—

DAISY: Am I?

AGNES: Yes.

DAISY: I saw you whispering. I saw you. Clicking your tongue in disappointment, and shrugging your shoulders, Mother. I saw you. I heard you. "Fritz and I just don't know how she got this way. And she won't let us help her", "We've tried everything", "We don't know what she does, but she sure scares those men off."... "By the way, do you know any single men? But, God knows, give her Prince Charming, and she'll probably throw him away too."

AGNES: Daisy—

DAISY: "Give her a frog to kiss and damned if nothing happens."

AGNES: I said no such thing—

DAISY: No?

AGNES: No. But there's certainly no harm in asking around—

DAISY: Stop! I don't want to be married! So stop! Just stop! You stop embarrassing me, Mother, and I'll stop embarrassing you. O K? Let's make a deal. We'll just call it a truce. You take the chip off your shoulder, and I'll stop crying on it. O K? You too, Daddy. You don't have to carry it. You're done. I'm alone and staying that way. You can rest in peace. You don't have to take care of me. It's not your fault. I'm alone. Live with it. Done.

DOCTOR TITTELS: Daisy—

DAISY: Come, Ruby.

(DAISY *pushes the baby carriage out the door.* RUBY *tries to put on her coat.*)

RUBY: I had a lovely time, Mister Tittels. Mister Tittels. I thought it was all very exciting.

DOCTOR TITTELS: Thank you, Ruby—

RUBY: And I really don't think the baby heard much of anything too racy. We're, we're going to church tomorrow anyway. I'm sure the Pastor will take care of it. *(She exits.)*

(Silence)

AGNES: Well.

EDGAR: Maybe I should go—

DOCTOR TITTELS: No, no. We won't let Daisy spoil our fun, now will we?

EDGAR: It is getting late—

DOCTOR TITTELS: We could play a game of chess? Do you like chess?

EDGAR: I don't play.

AGNES: If Edgar wants to go, Fritz, let him go—

DOCTOR TITTELS: But then Daisy will have ruined everything. I will not let her to ruin my night. I am too happy.

AGNES: Of course you are, dear—

DOCTOR TITTELS: We can play some music. How about that?

AGNES: It is getting late—

DOCTOR TITTELS: Music! *(He turns on the radio.)* Come Agnes, dance with me.

AGNES: I am tired.

DOCTOR TITTELS: Dance with me—

AGNES: What about Edgar? Are you just going to make him stay to watch us dance?

DOCTOR TITTELS: No, no. Of course not. We can all dance together. Come Edgar.

EDGAR: I do have to work in the morning—

DOCTOR TITTELS: One dance for your old professor.

AGNES: Fritz—

(DOCTOR TITTLES grabs them both around the waist.

DOCTOR TITTELS: Here we are. Dancing.

(DOCTOR TITTLES tries to move them to the music.)

AGNES: This isn't very comfortable, dear.

EDGAR: Maybe just the two of you should—

DOCTOR TITTELS: No, no. I like this. Feels very cozy, huh?

(They dance. DOCTOR TITTLES starts to feel dizzy.)

DOCTOR TITTELS: O K. I'm going to sit this one out... you two keep dancing.

AGNES: Dear, I—

(DOCTOR TITTLES stumbles to the radio.)

DOCTOR TITTELS: No, no. I want to watch you dance. Dance, with her, Edgar—

EDGAR: Sir, it is getting late—

DOCTOR TITTELS: Don't be silly. It's my party, isn't it?

AGNES: Fritz—

DOCTOR TITTELS: Dance. It's a lovely song. *(He turns up the radio.)* Dance.

(EDGAR *and* AGNES *dance.*)

(DOCTOR TITTLES *pushes them closer together.*)

DOCTOR TITTELS: She doesn't bite, Edgar. Now dance like you mean it.

AGNES: Fritz—

DOCTOR TITTELS: Sshh...you're missing the song... it's a love song.

(AGNES *and* EDGAR *dance closer.*)

(DOCTOR TITTLES *wanders over and falls on the couch.*)

DOCTOR TITTELS: I just love a love song.

(DOCTOR TITTLES *sits watching them dance.*)

(*Awkwardly,* AGNES *and* EDGAR *dance to the love song.*)

DOCTOR TITTELS: So romantic.

(*They continue dancing with* DOCTOR TITTLES *watching.*)

SCENE TWO:
THE BEDROOM

(*Two twin beds.* AGNES *and* DOCTOR TITTLES *lie in one bed together. He turns over, breathing heavily. She lies still.*)

AGNES: Good night, Fritz.

(DOCTOR TITTLES *stays beside* AGNES *in bed. She moves over a little.*)

AGNES: Fritz?

DOCTOR TITTELS: What?

(DOCTOR TITTLES *puts his arms around* AGNES.)

AGNES: It's—you're—it's a little crowded, dear.

DOCTOR TITTELS: Is it?

(AGNES *waits;* DOCTOR TITTLES *still doesn't climb into his own bed.*)

AGNES: Fritz?

DOCTOR TITTELS: What a success, huh? My book?

AGNES: Yes—yes, dear—

DOCTOR TITTELS: I am happy.

AGNES: Good—

DOCTOR TITTELS: I am a happy man.

(AGNES *doesn't move.*)

(*On the video screen, a distance from the camera, it's a blurry, sideways image of* JOY *and the cameraman [*DAN*] making love on the bed.*)

SCENE THREE:
MOTHER, PLEASE

(AGNES *vacuums the carpet.* DOCTOR TITTLES's *desk is clean and stacked with copies of his new book.*)

(AGNES *can't hear the knocking on the door.*)

(DAISY *lets herself in.*)

(AGNES *still doesn't see her.*)

(DAISY *quietly takes a seat at her father's desk. Staring. Saying nothing*)

(AGNES *turns off the vacuum cleaner and takes it to the kitchen. She enters with a feather duster and it's just then that she notices* DAISY *in the room.*)

DAISY: Hello Mother.

AGNES: I didn't hear you come in.

DAISY: I've come to return your tools.

AGNES: Finished the shelves then?

DAISY: Yes.

AGNES: That was nice of you, Daisy.

DAISY: Yes.

AGNES: Are you hungry?

DAISY: No.

AGNES: Are you sick?

DAISY: No.

AGNES: Shouldn't you be at school?

DAISY: Yes.

AGNES: Teachers' holiday?

DAISY: Not exactly.

AGNES: I hope you didn't just come over here to sulk, dear. I've got a lot of cleaning to do and I'm meeting your Aunt Ellen for tea later—

DAISY: Where's Daddy?

AGNES: He has a meeting with his publishers.

DAISY: Oh?

AGNES: They are scheduling interviews.

DAISY: I see.

AGNES: So if you've come to pick fights, you're shit out of luck.

DAISY: I didn't come for that.

(AGNES *dusts around* DAISY. DOCTOR TITTLES's *typewriter, the books.* DAISY *lifts her hands.*)

AGNES: I don't know how this house gets so messy with just your father and I—

DAISY: I'm in trouble, Mom.

AGNES: Now, please dear. Don't start one of your dramatic moments. I really don't like to keep my sister waiting—

DAISY: I think I'm in trouble at school.

AGNES: You never do go to those faculty meetings—

DAISY: No—

AGNES: And you're never on time. You could try and be more punctual, Daisy—

DAISY: This has nothing to do with time!

AGNES: Don't shout.

DAISY: *(Softer)* It's got nothing to do with that—

AGNES: You see there, the very first thing you do when you come in this house is start shouting, and you blame your father for giving you lectures and making you feel—

DAISY: Mother, please. Please. I, I've done something—could you please stop dusting?

AGNES: I've only got half an hour—

DAISY: Please!

(AGNES *stops dusting.)*

AGNES: Your temper is really—

DAISY: Mother. I...I.

(AGNES *waits.)*

DAISY: I tried to kiss one of my students.

AGNES: What?

DAISY: I kissed one of my students.

AGNES: You, you tried, or you did?

DAISY: I did. Kinda—

AGNES: Why?

DAISY: I don't know.

AGNES: You don't know? *(She waits.)*

DAISY: Well, I—

AGNES: What did he do—what did he say—did he tell one of the other teachers—

DAISY: No.

AGNES: What did he—

DAISY: She didn't.

AGNES: She? *(She sits down.)*

DAISY: I didn't mean to, Mother. I just, I don't know what...I just couldn't stop myself—

AGNES: Oh Daisy.

DAISY: I mean, she's just...she's just so beautiful. The most beautiful girl in the school. Really. Everyone thinks so.

AGNES: Daisy—

DAISY: And today, today she stayed after class to ask for some help on her paper, just some spelling and grammar questions and she smelled so nice, so very nice...like lost exotic flowers and—

AGNES: You couldn't stop yourself?

DAISY: No.

AGNES: What's wrong with you—

DAISY: Her hair was next to mine. Clean hair. Blond curls. Kinda long... And her cheek. Her smooth cheek. Lightly flushed. The kind of skin girls still have in high school...it's not fair how sweet it is, is it?

AGNES: I don't know—

DAISY: My lips were so close to her and she was so close that I thought I could just brush my lips against her cheek and she wouldn't notice, not really, but—

AGNES: Oh Daisy—

DAISY: But she turned and her lips were there instead. Perfect lips, Mother. Pink and full and gently parted. I couldn't stop myself. I, I just...I was pulled to them—

AGNES: Why?

DAISY: I wanted to touch them on mine. I just wanted to feel them on my lips.

AGNES: Daisy—

DAISY: But she turned. She turned away.

AGNES: And she told no one—

DAISY: I kissed her ear instead. *(She laughs in spite of herself.)*

AGNES: What did she do?

DAISY: She let me.

AGNES: Daisy—

DAISY: She has a beautiful ear.

AGNES: Why?

DAISY: I wanted to taste her. I just...I couldn't stop myself.

AGNES: You're her teacher.

DAISY: I know.

AGNES: What if she tells the principal, other teachers, students—

DAISY: She won't.

AGNES: How do you know? How do you know that?

DAISY: Because she wanted to be tasted.

AGNES: You're making excuses—

DAISY: She felt it too.

AGNES: You don't know that for sure. Oh, Daisy...
what's wrong with you?

DAISY: I'm in love, Mother.

AGNES: You are that girl's teacher. She is fifteen

DAISY: Sixteen—

AGNES: Think what could happen if anyone at your
school finds out.

DAISY: I'll be fired—

AGNES: And you think anyone's going to hire you
anywhere else?

DAISY: I just wanted to taste her skin, Mother. Just one
little taste. So young and hopeful and desired...I just
wanted to taste what that is—

AGNES: Stay away from her.

DAISY: She's the most beautiful girl in school and
I kissed her—

AGNES: I mean it, Daisy. She could ruin you.

(DAISY *laughs that odd laugh again.*)

DAISY: I know.

AGNES: Your father—

(DAISY *rushes to* AGNES.)

DAISY: Don't you dare tell him. Please—

AGNES: How can I keep this from him?

DAISY: I mean it. Please.

(DAISY *hugs* AGNES *tightly.*)

DAISY: You can't tell him. He'll put me in with a shrink and—

AGNES: She was a girl, Daisy!

DAISY: I won't do it again. I promise—

AGNES: She could ruin you—

DAISY: She won't.

AGNES: You've really done it this time.

DAISY: Don't tell Daddy. Please.

AGNES: You could be ruined.

DAISY: Just don't tell Daddy.

(On the video screen. JOY *lies under the sheets, looks at the camera)*

JOY: I won't tell.

SCENE FOUR

(Restaurant. DOCTOR TITTLES *sits alone, looking over a menu. Waiting)*

(He checks his watch, impatiently. There's a small stack of his books sitting on edge of the table.)

*(*EDGAR *enters, apologizing.)*

EDGAR: I am so sorry I'm late, Doctor Tittles. *(He offers his hand.)* Please please accept my apology. I didn't mean to keep you waiting. But I am absolutely swamped with patients these days.

DOCTOR TITTELS: No harm done, Edgar. Nice to see you—

EDGAR: Thank you, sir. Life can just move at a gloriously blistering pace sometimes, can't it?—

DOCTOR TITTELS: Your practice is flourishing?

EDGAR: I don't mean to brag, sir. But. Yes. I think
flourish might be exactly the right word. It's all the
recommendations. I've even had to turn patients
away—

DOCTOR TITTELS: Congratulations. *(He searches the
restaurant.)*

EDGAR: Ninety percent of my practice is women. Thank
God. Ninety percent. Wow...I couldn't imagine a better,
more satisfying life for myself, than this, sir—

DOCTOR TITTELS: This table's much too small—

EDGAR: Fascinating people, women. Don't you think?
...So many mysteries. Intriguing details. Beauty. Wow.
A diamond mine...

DOCTOR TITTELS: Yes.

EDGAR: And I really feel like I'm getting, like I *can* get,
to the *pith* of the human psyche.

(DOCTOR TITTLES searches the restaurant.)

EDGAR: It is so much more interesting to sit in an honest
session with a woman, and gently help unfold her, than
relentlessly tap away at the stubborn exterior of a man,
isn't it?

DOCTOR TITTELS: I haven't seen the waiter—

EDGAR: It's the difference between, say...water and
stone. Bird and elephant. Blue and black. Flesh and
bone. One *wishes* to be understood, yet cleverly keeps
you guessing, keeps you on your toes by slowly,
carefully letting you go deeper and deeper—the
woman, I'm talking about here, of course—

DOCTOR TITTELS: Uh huh—

EDGAR: While the other, the man, seems to constantly
wish to avoid any real understanding, thus keeps you
chasing your tail, or banging your head against the wall

like an asylum patient. Yes. A woman will simply let you inside her in ways that a man—at the risk of using an awful metaphor, sir—

DOCTOR TITTELS: I wrote a book on the subject, Edgar.

EDGAR: Of course! Of course, your fantastic book. You're the expert—

DOCTOR TITTELS: I know every inch of the female psyche. I know her well, Edgar. I have built a successful career on her. I've unlocked her desires. Blood, sweat, tears and brassieres, right here. *(He taps the books.)* Worth every minute.

EDGAR: I'm embarrassing myself...rambling on... sometimes I think I'm still trying to impress you, sir. I really do. Or. Could be intimidation.

DOCTOR TITTELS: Yes.

EDGAR: Yes...That wouldn't be surprising. Good old-fashioned intimidation.

DOCTOR TITTELS: Where's the waiter?

EDGAR: Could very well be intimidation *and* admiration at play. Uh huh. Father issues. Rearing their head. Hmmm. I know I've got them...maybe Mother issues too—Yes, well, Authority figures...desperately trying to please, impress...Hmm...Yes. That certainly would be natural.

DOCTOR TITTELS: Waiter?! Chairs?! We need more chairs here!

EDGAR: More chairs? I'm sorry, sir, but, why do we need—

DOCTOR TITTELS: For the others.

EDGAR: Others, sir?

DOCTOR TITTELS: Doctor Johannson, Doctor Roberts...
Doctor Hughes? Professor Gunther? Aren't they joining
us today?

EDGAR: I don't know.

DOCTOR TITTELS: I've invited them. Didn't they tell you?

EDGAR: No, sir.

DOCTOR TITTELS: No?

EDGAR: Not that I know of.

DOCTOR TITTELS: Are you sure?

EDGAR: I saw Doctor Hughes, and Doctor Roberts in the
office this morning, and neither mentioned it.

DOCTOR TITTELS: Oh.

EDGAR: Both were in sessions when I left.

DOCTOR TITTELS: Two more chairs then. For Doctor
Johannson and Professor Gunther—

EDGAR: I think they're out of town, sir. We play golf
on Fridays and they—

DOCTOR TITTELS: Why?

EDGAR: Away on vacation.

DOCTOR TITTELS: Oh.

EDGAR: Tropical cruises. I think.

DOCTOR TITTELS: Cruises.

EDGAR: I guess it's just the two of us. Doctor to doctor.

DOCTOR TITTELS: Yes.

EDGAR: Something the matter, sir?

DOCTOR TITTELS: No, no. I just thought they were
going to—I thought they might want to join us.
I signed copies of my book for all of you.

EDGAR: That's very thoughtful, sir.

(DOCTOR TITTLES *hands* EDGAR *one of the books.* EDGAR *reads inside the cover.*)

EDGAR: "To Doctor Bernard Hughes. I am honored to share my years of research and knowledge with my peers and coll—"

(DOCTOR TITTLES *rips it from* EDGAR's *hands.*)

DOCTOR TITTELS: That one is not for you—

(DOCTOR TITTLES *replaces it with another book from the stack. He checks it twice before he hands it to* EDGAR.)

EDGAR: "To my favorite student, Edgar. Read! Learn! Enjoy! Sincerely, Doctor Fritz Tittels." Wow. Very thoughtful. I will certainly treasure this. I know the perfect spot right on my shelf—

DOCTOR TITTELS: I can give them to the others another time.

EDGAR: I'm sure they will appreciate that.

DOCTOR TITTELS: Of course. (*He looks at his menu.*)

EDGAR: They most certainly will, sir. (*He takes the cue to look at his menu.*)

(*Silence*)

EDGAR: The prime rib is very good here. (*Silence*) It's really very good.

(*On the video screen,* JOY *is still under the covers.*)

DAN: (*O S*) Do you think sex is about happiness?

JOY: I think it's about a lot of things.

DAN: (*O S*) Passion?

JOY: I don't know. I'm not sure if I'd call it some kind of need for "passion"...not really...I can get passion

from a lot of things in my life...my work, my friends,
art, music...whatever...I think it's on some other level...

DAN: *(O S)* Physical.

JOY: Yeah, but I'd like to think it's bigger than that...
Older...deeper...transcendental..."mythological"?...

DAN: *(O S)* Help.

JOY: Hey, I hate all the long words and the kind of
pansy way people try and explain a basic human need
for connection...I do...but I do think it's a basic human
need to connect, with another person—

DAN: *(O S)* Physically.

JOY: Yes. But. It goes beyond that. I have this sense,
when I'm having sex, (Good sex)—

DAN: *(O S)* May I take that as a compliment?

JOY: I feel *pulled*...by some large, amazing, gigantic
force or...creature...maybe a bird...a big bird...
(and I'm not talking Sesame Street...more like a
condor or something) ...I mean, the size of this house...
(She spreads her arms.) You know, with some million foot
wingspan—

DAN: *(O S. Laughing)* Uh huh.

JOY: And—I'm serious—it's just calling me forth, and
I don't care where I am or what's going on in my life or
who I'm married to, or who he is married to, I just need
to feel it—I don't want to stop myself because life is too
short as it is—

DAN: *(O S)* Isn't that love?—

JOY: I'm just going to reach for that feeling, because
I don't want to stop and think and kill it, you know—

(KATIE walks in. Looks at her mother, then at the camera.)

KATIE: What are you doing?

JOY: Talking.

KATIE: Naked?

JOY: Yes...I always talk better naked.

KATIE: You don't even know him.

JOY: I do now.

SCENE FIVE

(AGNES *sits on the couch, staring into space. A cup of tea sits beside her*)

(DOCTOR TITTLES *enters. A little bored, looking for something to do in the house now that his book is finished*)

DOCTOR TITTELS: You want to watch television?

(AGNES *is quiet.*)

DOCTOR TITTELS: Agnes?

AGNES: Yes, dear?

DOCTOR TITTELS: You want to watch television? (*He reaches to turn it on.*)

AGNES: Not now.

DOCTOR TITTELS: No?

AGNES: No.

DOCTOR TITTELS: Why not?

AGNES: I'm not in the mood, dear.

DOCTOR TITTELS: Oh. O K. (*He looks around the room. Picks up his book*) You want to read?

AGNES: No.

(DOCTOR TITTLES *looks around, aimless.*)

DOCTOR TITTELS: What do you want to do?

AGNES: I just want to sit here.

(*Finally* DOCTOR TITTLES *sits down beside her on the couch. Quiet. Looks around the room. Bored*)

DOCTOR TITTELS: Daisy call?

AGNES: No.

(DOCTOR TITTLES *nods, thinks about that.*)

DOCTOR TITTELS: Maybe I should call her. (*He looks at his watch.*) I'll call her tomorrow. (*He takes a pen and small pad of paper out of his front pocket and carefully writes that down.*) "Call Daisy." (*He inspects it, as part of his list of "things to do". Taps his head with the pad, then puts it back in his pocket. Only to remember:*) What's her number? (*He grabs the pad of paper again to write it down.*)

AGNES: It's in the kitchen, dear.

(DOCTOR TITTLES *puts the pad back in his pocket.*)

DOCTOR TITTELS: I can get it later. (*Silence*) I'll get it later. (*Silence*) That was a very good dinner.

AGNES: Thank you.

DOCTOR TITTELS: I'm full.

(AGNES *nods her head at* DOCTOR TITTLES, *agreeing.*)

(*He moves closer to her and puts his arm around her.*)

DOCTOR TITTELS: You're a good cook.

AGNES: I know.

DOCTOR TITTELS: Delicious as always.

(AGNES *smiles at* DOCTOR TITTLES, *continues staring off in space.*)

DOCTOR TITTELS: You spoil me. (*He touches her hair, her cheek.*) You're a beautiful woman, Agnes. Just as beautiful as the day we met.

AGNES: Don't be silly.

DOCTOR TITTELS: I'm not being silly. *(He turns her face to his.)* It's true. *(He holds her face in his hands.)* Look at you.

(On the video screen, JOY *dresses.)*

DAN: *(O S)* Isn't that— *(He sneezes O S.)* I think there's just a lot of...do you ever dust?

JOY: No.

DAN: *(O S)* I can tell. You never answered my question. Isn't that feeling, love?

JOY: Just put your pants on, Sneezy.

DAN: *(O S)* C'mon—

JOY: I thought you wanted to talk about sex.

SCENE SIX

(The TITTELS *living room)*

*(*DOCTOR TITTLES' *desk is covered with a larger stack of his books.)*

*(*RUBY *reads from a copy.)*

RUBY: "It is now clear that it is up to the American woman to create her own sexual revolution. She must take the future into her own hands. With unrelenting courage and conviction, she must claim her right to Love and to be sexually fulfilled: to have the life she knows to be truly her own."

*(*AGNES *enters.)*

RUBY: "However, monogamy and marriage still remain the only guarantee for love, a happy and satisfied life, and the only structure upon which a healthy society can truly rest—

AGNES: Ruby—

RUBY: "While monogamy does impose many restrictions on both sexes, its attributes far outweigh its detriments. Security is paramount, and nothing lasting can be built without a firm, steadfast commitment from one partner to another. Where commitment wanes, chaos ensues. Once chaos begins, there's no stopping its wrath upon human emotions."...This is fascinating. *(She begins to find another passage.)*

AGNES: You can take it home and read it.

RUBY: Huh?

AGNES: You can have it.

RUBY: Really? I hope my husband doesn't think I'm a sex crazy or something... *(She thumbs through more of the book.)*

AGNES: Thank you for stopping by.

RUBY: I know how you love to see the baby.

AGNES: And thank you for the casserole. That was very sweet of you.

RUBY: You're welcome. I've got plenty... *(She continues to read.)*

AGNES: I'm really not feeling completely well, dear, and I've got a million things to do—

(RUBY looks up. Finally closes the book)

RUBY: Oh, I am sorry, Mrs Tittels. Can I get you anything?

AGNES: No, no. I'm fine.

RUBY: Is it a cold?

AGNES: No.

RUBY: Flu?

AGNES: I just, I suppose I just don't feel myself, dear.

RUBY: Headache?

AGNES: Some.

RUBY: Body ache?

AGNES: Yes. A little—

RUBY: You're sure it's not a flu?

AGNES: I don't think so, dear. (*She opens the door.*)

RUBY: You want to hold the baby?

AGNES: I shouldn't—

RUBY: It might make you feel better.

AGNES: Maybe I'll just go to bed. For a little while—

RUBY: No, no. Please. Hold the baby first, Mrs Tittels. I know how happy she makes you.

AGNES: I've got so much to do, Ruby—

(RUBY *takes the baby from the carriage and puts it in* AGNES's *arms.*)

RUBY: She's such a good sleepyhead. Hold her and you'll feel worlds better. I always do.

(AGNES *takes the baby in her arms.*)

RUBY: Anytime I'm feeling low, I just look at my baby and I don't think I feel it anymore. I don't. All I see is her...and I start to think about what I can do to make her happy...what she needs...not old selfish little me... Strange...I forget why I was sad then...children just take it all away, don't they?

AGNES: I suppose so.

(RUBY *and* AGNES *stare at the baby.* AGNES *begins to cry.*)

RUBY: Oh dear. Don't cry, Mrs Tittels. (*She touches* AGNES's *cheek.*) Don't cry. You're just having a bad day.

(AGNES *nods.*)

RUBY: We all have them.

(On the video screen, JOY *brushes her hair, begins to put on lipstick. Loud music plays in the background.)*

JOY: If she got pregnant now? At this age... She'd get an abortion. It would be her choice, of course... *(Smiles)* But she'd get an abortion. *(Yells to the other room)* Turn it down!

DAN: *(O S)* Would that be her choice or yours?

JOY: You think I'm controlling?

DAN: *(O S)* Maybe.

JOY: Well, I am her mother.

SCENE SEVEN:
FAMILY SAFETY

(Bedroom)

*(*EDGAR *waits. Checks his watch)*

*(*AGNES *rushes in.)*

AGNES: I'm so sorry—

EDGAR: I was getting worried.

AGNES: Nothing to worry about. No. *(She quickly sits down. Out of breath. Quickly touches his face.)* Hello, Edgar.

EDGAR: Hello—

AGNES: Have you had a nice day?

EDGAR: Yes—

AGNES: That's good. Yes.

EDGAR: How are you?—

AGNES: You look so handsome.

EDGAR: Do I?

AGNES: Heavens. (*She wipes her eye.*)

EDGAR: Are you O K?

AGNES: Just some dust. I was in such a hurry. I don't like to keep you waiting.

EDGAR: You're worth the wait. Let me get you some tea or something—

AGNES: Vodka.

EDGAR: Are you all right, Agnes?

AGNES: Oh fine. Just fine. How are you?

EDGAR: I'm well—

AGNES: Good. Good... You are a wonderful man, aren't you? Kind. Generous... Brilliant.

EDGAR: Oh the flattery.

(AGNES *wipes her eyes.*)

EDGAR: Maybe I should get some tea—

AGNES: How much do you love me, Edgar?

EDGAR: Pardon?

AGNES: Maybe you should get some vodka.

(EDGAR *begins to stand.*)

AGNES: How much do you love me?

(EDGAR *sits.*)

EDGAR: I'm not sure why you're asking—
does it matter—

AGNES: I could use a drink.

(EDGAR *begins to stand again.*)

AGNES: You know how I feel about you, don't you?

(EDGAR *sits.*)

EDGAR: Well, I have assumed you felt the same—

AGNES: Of course I do.

EDGAR: Good.

AGNES: I can't begin to tell you how you've changed me. I'm not the same woman I was a year ago. I have felt more for you...mercy, it is love—oh, this is a time for a drink—

(EDGAR *begins to stand.*)

AGNES: But you know it's not the same love as a mother's love.

(EDGAR *sits.*)

EDGAR: Of course not.

AGNES: No.

EDGAR: I wouldn't want you to love me like your child.

AGNES: Of course not.

EDGAR: No.

AGNES: It's very different.

EDGAR: Of course.

AGNES: I do many things for you.

EDGAR: I think so.

AGNES: Risk my marriage.

EDGAR: Yes—

AGNES: My reputation.

EDGAR: I would do the same for you, Agnes

AGNES: My heart—

EDGAR: I do love you. I would do—

AGNES: But a mother will do anything for her child.

EDGAR: Well, yes, I suppose.

AGNES: Yes.

EDGAR: It's natural.

AGNES: Yes.

EDGAR: Instinct.

AGNES: I think so—

(EDGAR *tries to touch* AGNES'*s hand.*)

EDGAR: Are you all right, Agnes—

AGNES: She'll sacrifice anything.

EDGAR: Maybe—

AGNES: Even herself.

EDGAR: If, if she must—

AGNES: She wants her child to be happy.

EDGAR: Of course.

AGNES: Safe.

EDGAR: Yes.

AGNES: At all costs.

EDGAR: Well—

AGNES: She will do anything to make sure her child is safe.

EDGAR: Agnes?

AGNES: Anything.

EDGAR: Agnes?

AGNES: I would like a drink, Edgar.

(EDGAR *begins to stand.*)

AGNES: How much do you love me?

(EDGAR *sits.*)

(*On the video screen,* JOY *sits with a photo album on her lap, turning pages...showing some of the photos to the camera.*)

JOY: My van...George...stranger...my first husband...
Carl, my second husband....boyfriend whose name
I can't remember...stranger...Texan...Harvard grad...
his car...mysterious Spaniard...his back...he had a nice
back...That's Katie as a baby. *(Yelling to the other room)*
When she was still cute! *(She turns the page)*

(The video freezes.)

SCENE EIGHT:
CONCLUSION

(The living room)

*(DOCTOR TITTLES wears a Hawaiian lei around his neck as
he pours champagne into glasses.)*

DOCTOR TITTELS: Lots of sun, huh?

*(EDGAR and DAISY stand in tropical wear, a bit more tanned
than before.)*

EDGAR: Not a cloud in the sky.

DAISY: Nope.

DOCTOR TITTELS: Pineapple? Did you get fresh
pineapple in the room?

DAISY: It was rotten—

EDGAR: That room you got us was very nice, sir.
Really first class.

(Silence)

DOCTOR TITTELS: Was it a good view?

DAISY: We had quite a view.

EDGAR: You could see for miles.

(Silence)

DOCTOR TITTELS: You see any whales?

EDGAR: No, no I don't think we did—

DAISY: They don't have whales out there, Daddy.

DOCTOR TITTELS: What do they have?

DAISY: Waves. Lots and lots of waves.

DOCTOR TITTELS: I see...I guess...the Pacific is a big ocean...lots of waves there.

(Silence)

*(*AGNES *enters from the kitchen, also wearing a lei, and carrying a tray of snacks.)*

AGNES: I know these appetizers aren't fresh from the sea, like you're used to now...but I hope they'll do. I've got more in the oven.

DAISY: They call these poo poos in Hawaii.

AGNES: Oh my.

DAISY: We ate a lot of poo poo, didn't we Edgar?

EDGAR: Yes. We did.

DAISY: Poo poos...and then there's muumuus.

EDGAR: We brought you a muumuu, Mrs Tittels.

AGNES: What's that?

DAISY: It's a blue dress.

AGNES: I like blue.

DAISY: Edgar picked it out.

AGNES: Well then...thank you, Edgar.

EDGAR: Yes. I thought...

(Silence)

DOCTOR TITTELS: Who would have thought, my young man, Edgar, back when you were my best and brightest student, that you'd be standing here, my very own son-in-law.

EDGAR: Who would have thought.

DOCTOR TITTELS: Not me.

(Silence)

EDGAR: Things change.

DOCTOR TITTELS: And change indeed. Right, Agnes?

AGNES: Well, I don't know—

DOCTOR TITTELS: I didn't see it coming, did you? ...Love was blooming right under my nose and I didn't even see it, did you, Agnes?

(Silence)

DAISY: What this party needs is some music. Right, Mother?

AGNES: That would be nice—

DOCTOR TITTELS: I didn't know you had it in you Daisy.

(DAISY turns on the radio. Bing Crosby's Where The Blue Of The Night... *plays.)*

DOCTOR TITTELS: I must be losing my touch. All these months writing, and I'm afraid I've lost my personal touch.... You think I'm losing my touch, Agnes?

AGNES: I don't know, dear.

DOCTOR TITTELS: I should see the signs of love.

AGNES: I should check the oven.

DAISY: Let me.

AGNES: Don't be silly. You sit and enjoy—

DAISY: You sit. I've been sitting for two weeks. *(She turns up the music as she exits to the kitchen.)*

DOCTOR TITTELS: You only marry once... Right? *(Silence)* We could use some more champagne. Get this party going. That wedding was so fast, and with Daisy puking in the aisles every five steps, I barely had a chance to eat a piece of cake, much less get drunk, huh?

AGNES: I'll get it—

DOCTOR TITTELS: No, no. Let me. I want to get the good stuff. I have it hidden. *(He exits.)*

(AGNES and EDGAR stand staring at each other as the song plays. Pulled, but they remain in place.)

(DAISY enters.)

DAISY: These are a little burnt.

(DOCTOR TITTLES enters.)

DOCTOR TITTELS: Here we are. Everyone bring their glasses here. We must toast to our happy new family.

AGNES: I think I've had enough, dear.

EDGAR: I'm really not—

DAISY: Hand me the bottle, Daddy—

DOCTOR TITTELS: No. Now. Everyone come here. Gather together. *(He pours champagne into everyone's glasses.)* Let a happy German man enjoy his fruitful, American life, for one little minute, will you?..Look at me!

(They look at him. DOCTOR TITTLES grabs a copy of his book.)

DOCTOR TITTELS: A successful book... *(He kisses the book, and puts his arm around AGNES.)* A devoted wife. *(He kisses her cheek.)* A married daughter. The surprise to beat all surprises there.

DAISY: Thanks, Daddy.

DOCTOR TITTELS: And best of all, a man, a son-in-law to beat all son-in-laws—

EDGAR: Thank you—

DOCTOR TITTELS: Right, Agnes?

AGNES: Yes, dear.

DOCTOR TITTELS: So. My new son. Ladies. *(He raises his glass to toast.)* To the future.

AGNES, EDGAR, DAISY: *(Out of sync)* To, to the future.

(Everyone drinks. An awkward silence prevails among them, but the song continues to play.)

(On the video screen, JOY sits with a photo album on her lap...she continues through photos.)

JOY: My father, Jim...my mother, Ruby...Ruby and me...and oops... *(She turns the pages quickly)* Me in some of my more compromising poses and positions... with the only real—my only real true love... *(She touches the pictures...)*

DAN: *(O S)* Can I see?

JOY: Oh, you want to see those, do you?... *(Smiles)*

DAN: *(O S)* Yes—

JOY: You'll have to turn off the camera for that.

DAN: *(O S)* Why?

JOY: Because that's private...

(Video screen goes to black.)

END OF PLAY

www.ingramcontent.com/pod-product-compliance
Lightning Source LLC
Chambersburg PA
CBHW052159090426
42741CB00010B/2333